GO FISH

What Others are Saying

"I have known Shonn for more than two decades. We have done life together, ministry together, and our families have grown together. I must say when it comes to sharing Jesus personally (personal evangelism) with people, Shonn is most passionate and capable. I have watched him as a husband, father, friend, and fellow Christ follower reach out to all circles and layers of people with his story of life change that Jesus did for him personally and how God desires that same change for all. If you are looking for answers on how to share your own Jesus story and be inspired to do so this is a must read!"

—Clay NeSmith
Lead Pastor, Barefoot Church
North Myrtle Beach, South Carolina

"Shonn has delivered another important resource for the modern church that is both timely and timeless. With rare authenticity and candor that only comes from one whose passion for personal evangelism exceeds his personal pride, Shonn examines his own ministry as a case study for personal evangelism in the local church.

In his quest to reconcile reality to divine calling, Shonn offers a roadmap for church leaders to clearly define reality and develop a strategy to courageously lead a church into the future that fully embraces God's missional design.

This resource equips students, encourages pastors, and empowers the church to Go Fish for the glory of God!"

—Tripp Atkinson
Associate Pastor, Sugar Hill Church
Sugar Hill, Georgia

"Passionate, Practical, and Motivating. This is how I would describe Shonn's heart and wisdom for personal evangelism. His life is his message, and his message is reaching people with the good news of Jesus Christ. His years of experience in evangelism and traveling all over the world have given him a laboratory in evangelism few of us get and insights even fewer of us would ever think to attain. This book is a must read and more importantly a must do!"

—Mickie Kelly
Pastor, NorthRidge Fellowship
Jerome, Idaho

"Keels' work demonstrates the kind of passion and creativity Christians need today to reach people for Christ."

—Brad Arnett, Ph.D.
Professor of New Testament and Greek,
Luther Rice Seminary
Atlanta, Georgia

"As a believer in Christ, this book encourages me to engage in the process of making disciples. As a senior pastor, this book shows me how I can build a church of disciple makers. As a seminary student, this book is a road map for me on how to research and write a ministry project that will make a difference beyond the classroom and that can be easily applied in any church context."

—Cesar Arocha
Pastor, Dallas Bay Church
Hixson, Tennessee

"Having worked with Shonn for decades, I can attest his calling for sharing the gospel is his passion. His experience preaching around the world to different people groups not many evangelists have the opportunity to reach gives him a unique insight. Shonn shows us that modern times are among us, but the gospel is timeless and personal evangelism should always be an integral part of our Christian walk."

— **Brandon Hensley**
President and Co-Founder, Team Impact Ministries
Dallas, Texas

"This book will motivate and move you toward personal evangelism."

—**Chip Minton**
International Evangelist
2-time U.S. Olympian, and former WCW Wrestler
Pensacola, Florida

"I have had the privilege of knowing Shonn for over 15 years and one of the things I admire about him is his constant commitment to personal evangelism! It is one thing for a pastor to preach about the importance of personal evangelism from behind a pulpit; it is another thing for him to put it into practice in his personal life. Shonn practices what he preaches so rest assured the truths shared in this book aren't just theory on paper, they are biblical principles he consistently lives out!"

— **Jared Douglas**
Lead Pastor, First Baptist Church
Red Oak, Texas

"In an age when evangelism is not only misunderstood, but often unpracticed, Shonn helps put the pieces together. The heart of this book is the very heart of the gospel! His encouragement, instruction, and gospel challenge are second to none!"

— **Jayson Hoagland**
Pastor, First Baptist Church
Wright City, Missouri

"I've had the pleasure of serving with Shonn for over 20 years sharing the gospel around the world. His knowledge and experience in personal evangelism is an incredible resource that should be taught and shared with all believers in the Lord Jesus Christ!"

— **Berry Handley**
International Evangelist
Indiana Wrestling Hall of Fame
Griffith, Indiana

"In this dynamic book, Shonn addresses what many see as the most important problem facing the modern church in America. Shonn carefully outlines underlying reasons for the problem and then offers practical solutions that you can use in your life and church to overcome this problem."

— **Lynn Myers, M.D.**
Deacon, The First Church
Oklahoma City, Oklahoma

"*Go Fish* was written out of Shonn's life experience as he has been boldly sharing Christ and equipping others to do the same for many years. To be around Shonn is to be encouraged to share your faith and, in this book, Shonn gives a practical and helpful plan written to be benefit every Christian and every local church in America and around the globe. This book is both helpful and encouraging!"

— **Bob Shelton**
Pastoral Coach and Consultant, Edify Leaders
Oklahoma City, Oklahoma

"I have known Shonn for more than two decades as a friend and a co-laborer in sharing Christ around the world. In this book, Shonn has distilled his vast Biblical knowledge to encourage and equip this generation to pursue a life where we look for opportunities to engage the lost. Unfortunately, many believers do not take seriously the Biblical mandate to "make disciples." I encourage you to read this challenging book to get equipped and motivated to share your faith!"

— **Jeffery J. Neal**
Associate Pastor of Discipleship and Missions,
Gracepointe Church
Co-Author of *Hold the Rope:
Having a Heart for the Lost*
Denton, Texas

"One of the major challenges to any evangelistic process is creating a desire within a person to actually share his faith with others. This work provides an intentional, step-by-step process by which churches can disciple others with the goal of increasing not only their knowledge of how to share the Gospel, but also the desire to share the Gospel. By not bifurcating discipling from evangelizing, this process can become an ongoing and seamless opportunity for followers of Christ to regularly experience the joy of sharing their faith with others."

— **Rusty Ricketson, D.Min., Ph.D.**

Master of Arts in Leadership Program Coordinator
and Professor, Luther Rice Seminary
Atlanta, Georgia

"'Go therefore and make disciples' (Mt. 28:19). These are the words of the Lord Jesus that challenge all believers to *Go Fish*. In this book, Shonn is fulfilling this command, TO GO AND TELL, and encouraging the church to do the same. This book will inspire, challenge, and convict you to be mindful of Christ's epic call, to go make disciples!"

— **Guy Earle**

President, Think Twice Ministries
Denton, Texas

"*Go Fish* is fruit from a dissertation by Shonn that brings the power of Christ's Call, prayer, and the Holy Spirit to refocus the believer's vision and the church's ministry back to the main thing of sharing the gospel. May the fruit of this book move us out of the tradition of church and into the practice of being the church. As Jesus prays, "that all of them may be one, Father, just as you are in me and I am in you. May they also be in us so that the world may believe that you have sent me" (Jn. 17:21)."

— **Vance McCollom, M.D.**

Deacon, The First Church
Oklahoma City, Oklahoma

"The current evangelical landscape appears to be increasingly fragmented and rudderless. Church attenders are confused regarding what living out the Gospel should look like because their pastors and other spiritual leaders appear confused. Presently evangelicalism is faced with diverse issues of an awakened culture with technological advances and Covid virus challenges on one hand and the social gospel on the other. In the midst of this ecclesiastical confusion, Shonn offers the wandering reader a clear, concise, practical, and thorough Biblical guide, calling the confused church back to its primary mission of disciple making."

— **James Austin, D.Min.**
Executive Director,
South Carolina Baptist Convention,
Retired
Columbia, South Carolina

GO
FISH

REVIVING PERSONAL EVANGELISM

SHONN KEELS

NASHVILLE

NEW YORK • LONDON • MELBOURNE • VANCOUVER

GO FISH
REVIVING PERSONAL EVANGELISM

© 2022 SHONN KEELS

Published in New York, New York, by Morgan James Publishing. Morgan James is a trademark of Morgan James, LLC. www.MorganJamesPublishing.com

A **FREE** ebook edition is available for you or a friend with the purchase of this print book.

CLEARLY SIGN YOUR NAME ABOVE

Instructions to claim your free ebook edition:
1. Visit MorganJamesBOGO.com
2. Sign your name CLEARLY in the space above
3. Complete the form and submit a photo of this entire page
4. You or your friend can download the ebook to your preferred device

ISBN 978-1-63195-575-4 paperback
ISBN 978-1-63195-576-1 ebook
Library of Congress Control Number:
2021905174

Cover Design by:
Rachel Lopez
www.r2cdesign.com

Morgan James is a proud partner of Habitat for Humanity Peninsula and Greater Williamsburg. Partners in building since 2006.

Get involved today! Visit
MorganJamesPublishing.com/giving-back

A Doctor of Ministry Project

Personal Evangelism:

A Return to a New Testament Model of Reaching People

Michael Shonn Keels

DM 9500: Doctoral Ministry Project

Doctoral Ministry Project

Approval Sheet

Candidate: Michael Shonn Keels

Degree: Doctor of Ministry

Title of Composition: Personal Evangelism: A Return to a New Testament Model of Reaching People

Purpose of Composition: The purpose of this project is to specifically examine the young adults at The First Church with particular reference to their lack of attention to and engagement in personal evangelism in order to develop a church-wide personal evangelism training ministry to be sponsored, led, and conducted by the project director.

Academic Committee

Dr. Ron Cobb

Major Professor

Dr. Brad Arnett

Graduate Committee

Dr. Rusty Ricketson

Graduate Committee

February 2020

Date Approved

TABLE OF CONTENTS

Acknowledgments

I thank my God and Savior the Lord Jesus Christ for saving me and setting me apart for a life of service to Him. Because of Your grace I am forever changed!

Bonnie, you are my best friend and the love of my life. I am blessed to be on this journey with you. Thank you for your patience with me, your love for me, and for your constant encouragement as I seek to honor God in life and ministry. Your listening ear, wise counsel, and tasty snacks along the way helped make this work possible.

Brelin, Bryce, and Baylee, one of my greatest privileges is being the patriarch of our family. You all make my job easy. Your love for the Lord and your passion for His mission to reconcile the world to Himself are contagious.

Bob Shelton, thank you for your editorial work. You are a great brother!

The First Church, you are a great church and a generous people. Thank you for supporting and encouraging my passion for professional development and personal evangelism. Thank you also for being the laboratory for the experiment that made this project possible. Your commitment to spiritual growth and desire to invite others on this great journey are commendable. You are a great church.

To the control group, the focus group, and my Bible study group, thank you for playing a significant role in helping make this project a success. The value of your participation in this project is incalculable. I am forever grateful!

Thank you, David Hancock and the amazing team at Morgan James who helped make this book a reality. Y'all are awesome!

Finally, thank you to the many others who helped me realize that one of the greatest ways we can honor God is to be obedient to His "Great Commission." Your commitment to Jesus and to making Him known have inspired me to be more faithful and fruitful in my own life and witness.

FOREWORD

I first met Shonn Keels a number of years ago on a Delta flight from Atlanta, Georgia to Dallas, Texas. We only remained strangers for a short time. As God in His providence would have it, we quickly discovered that Shonn was a student at the educational institution where I was a professor. Over the course of the flight, Shonn shared about his love for Jesus, his excitement with the evangelistic ministry in which he was currently involved, and his academic preparation for future ministry. It turned out to be one of the best flights I have ever experienced! It was thrilling to discover a new friend and follower of Jesus, but the story would not end there.

Fast forward to a number of years later. I was pleased when I discovered that Shonn had completed graduate school and was applying for admission to the Doctor of Ministry program that I now coordinated. Throughout the next several years, I watched Shonn grow—he developed spiritually, ministerially, and academically. When the time came for Shonn to write his

Doctor of Ministry Project (dissertation), it was my privilege to serve as his major academic advisor. Through many months of rigorous work Shonn honed, edited, and rewrote his Project into an exemplary document that he successfully defended in February 2020. Luther Rice Seminary awarded Dr. Shonn Keels the Doctor of Ministry degree in May 2020.

The book that you are about to read represents a life well lived to the glory of God. The impetus for this book is Shonn's Doctor of Ministry Project. You will quickly see that Shonn has the heart of a pastor, the soul of an evangelist, and the mind of a scholar. As you invest your time in reading this book, you will realize at least three things. First, this book is *unwaveringly evangelistic*. Shonn is keenly aware that Christians today are sometimes intimidated by a post-Christian culture and wary of sharing their faith with others. The author effectively motivates the reader to reveal the gospel to those in need of Christ. Next, this resource is *uncompromisingly biblical*. This book rests on the sure foundation of the Word of God. Dr. Keels skillfully uses Scripture to reinforce to the reader the imperative of evangelism in the 21st century. Finally, this book is *unapologetically academic*. True scholarship is always applicable to real life. I believe that you will find this book intensely practical and imminently useful in sharing Jesus Christ with others.

I pray that almighty God will use this volume to help you point others to their need for Jesus Christ. In the magnificent words of Ephesians 4:11-12: *"And He gave some as apostles, and some as prophets, and some as evangelists, and some as pastors and teachers, for the equipping of the saints for the work of service, to the building up of the body of Christ.*" May God do great things through you as you are obedient to Him is my prayer.

—Ron Cobb, Ph.D.
Coordinator of the Doctor of Ministry Degree Program
Luther Rice Seminary

PREFACE

Why another book on evangelism? This is a great question that deserves an honest answer even if it hurts. **First**, we need another book on personal evangelism because many who make up the evangelical church in North America today are living in direct disobedience to the Great Commission given by the Lord Jesus Christ. All experts who study the evangelistic efforts of those who make up the local church agree that only a small percentage of Christians are personally sharing their faith on a consistent basis. This is sadly unacceptable! A return to a New Testament model of people personally reaching people is necessary. *Go Fish: Reviving Personal Evangelism* is an answer that will help prepare people for personal evangelism.

Second, we need another book on personal evangelism for the evangelical church that includes a culturally relevant training ministry manual that can be used by any local church in America and beyond. The appendices in this book alone can serve any church that desires to prepare an army of people for personal evangelism. **A step-by-step plan for growing both faithful and fruitful disciples of the Lord Jesus is included.** One of the primary goals of this project was to build something that would be transferable. This goal has been met and the contents within *Go Fish: Reviving Personal Evangelism* can be easily reproduced in any church.

Finally, we need a book like this one for the seminary student who is wrestling with the tall order of writing a doctoral ministry project--dissertation. The process for the seminary student is arduous and can be overwhelming. *Go Fish: Reviving Personal Evangelism* includes an actual Doctor of Ministry Project from front to finish. The entire project is presented in an easy-to-read fashion to help ministry students better understand how to build a God-honoring project that can be implemented in any church at any time. If you are a student and you want help as you prayerfully put your Doctoral Ministry Project together feel free to reach out to me at shonnkeels@gmail.com.

Please take note, the name of the actual church studied has been withheld and changed to The First Church or TFC.

Blessings on your journey!

—**Shonn Keels**

INTRODUCTION

The first and last words of Jesus were the same, *Go Fish*. In Matthew 4:19 with the calling of His first disciples and in Matthew 28:18-20 with his farewell message to His disciples, Jesus calls and commissions His followers to *Go Fish*. Fishing does not happen by accident. Catherine Renfro agrees, "We must intentionally look for ways to make Jesus known to those we meet."[1] Yes, we must be INTENTIONAL! The gospel message is too important to be left untold. The gospel is preeminent! William Wilson writes, "In the Bible the Gospel of Jesus Christ is described as the most important thing in all the world."[2] The apostle Paul supports this declaration as he writes in his letter to the Corinthian church that the gospel is of "first importance"[3] (1 Cor. 15:3). The gospel is of first importance; yet it is often the

1 Catherine Renfro, "5 Steps to Starting Gospel Conversations." On mission magazine, (winter 2021): 6.

2 Dr. William Wilson, "Engaging the World: A Basic Introduction to Evangelism." www.projectfocus.education. (Lesson #1).

3 All Scripture quotations unless otherwise noted are taken from the New International Version Bible found at www.bible.com.

most neglected. Gene Edwards agrees, "It is just that the most powerful and necessary concept of Christianity is still dead!"[4] Personal evangelism must be resurrected in the local church. It is the church the Lord Jesus crafted and commissioned to reach the world with the good news that Jesus saves (Eph. 2:10 & Mt. 28:18-20). Wilson concurs, "We were designed for evangelism."[5] There is only one thing required of the Christian he can do on earth that he cannot do in heaven—share the gospel with a lost person. If this is to happen today, we need a *Revival in Personal Evangelism.*

The challenge is, the membership of The First Church Church (TFC) is not actively engaged in sharing the gospel of the Lord Jesus Christ. Personal evangelism is no longer the priority of many in the church. In this context, the majority of the membership has become comfortable with doing church rather than being the church. The purpose of this project is to examine the young adults at TFC with particular reference to their lack of attention to and engagement in personal evangelism in order to develop a church-wide personal evangelism training ministry to be sponsored, led, and conducted by the project director, Shonn Keels, who serves in the pastoral ministry. This project is vital for TFC considering its conversion growth is low and its growth by transfers is high (See Appendix A). Overall, the church is experiencing great growth; but it is not the result of the engagement of the membership in personal evangelism. This is unacceptable. Ray Stanford writes, "There

---

4   Gene Edwards, *How to Have a Soul Winning Church.* (Springfield, Missouri: Gospel Publishing House): 14.

5   Dr. William Wilson, "Engaging the World: A Basic Introduction to Evangelism." www.projectfocus.education. (Lesson #2).

is an urgent need for men and women to dedicate themselves to the important task of becoming specialists in soul winning!"[6] Personal evangelism is the right and responsibility of all who claim Christ as Savior. John R. Rice agrees, "Every Christian ought to be a soul winner."[7] There are no exceptions! This project addresses the growing lack of zeal for personally reaching people and the lack of participation in personal evangelism among the church populace. TFC does not appear to be the lone church in this struggle to engage people in soul winning. The struggle is ubiquitous. Alphonse Turner agrees, "One of the most difficult areas of any church is the ministry of evangelism."[8] Personal evangelism is not the priority of the church in America. George Godfrey concurs, "The majority of God's people are silent about Christ."[9] Godfrey continues, "… approximately 95 percent of all Christians never witness for Christ."[10] This lackadaisical attitude toward personal evangelism is both alarming and disheartening. This author believes there are a number of reasons for this lack of zeal for and this lack of participation in personal evangelism within the church today. The most significant reasons will be discussed in this book.

---

6   Dr. A. Ray Stanford, *Handbook of Personal Evangelism*. (Pharr, Texas: Wally Marillo, 1999): 4.

7   John R. Rice, *The Golden Path to Successful Soul Winning*. (Murfreesboro, Tennessee: The Sword of The Lord Publishers, 1961): 45.

8   Alphonse Turner Jr., "A Personal Evangelism Training Plan" (Doctoral diss. Temple Baptist Seminary, Fayetteville, North Carolina, 201

9   George Godfrey, *How to Win Souls and Influence People for Heaven*. (Grand Rapids, Michigan: Baker Book House, 1973): 18.

10   Ibid., 16.

The church in America is facing greater challenges today than perhaps ever before in the history of the United States. George Barna writes, "Rates of church attendance, religious affiliation, belief in God, prayer and Bible-reading have all been dropping for decades. By consequence, the role of religion in public life has been slowly diminishing, and the church no longer functions with the cultural authority it held in times past."[11] This is not good! Bill Hybels writes, "The local church is the hope of the world."[12] Hybels is correct. The church is to be the hope of the world in that she has the only Answer—Jesus! Tom Clegg and Warren Bird add, "The way Christians do church today is the equivalent of ignoring millions of desperate, but unrecognized, cries for help."[13] Considering the current state of the church, the indifferent spiritual climate, and the darkness that ensues, the church must lovingly confront these growing challenges head on. Among these challenges, the one that rises to the top is personal evangelism.

Personal evangelism, or the lack thereof, is one of the greatest challenges of the church today. Fewer Christians are personally engaged in sharing their faith with lost people. Thom Rainer agrees, "We Christians have become disobedient and lazy."[14] Rainer continues, "The sad reality we discovered

11   George Barna, "The Most Post-Christian Cities in America: 2017." https://www.barna.com/research/post-christian-cities-america-2017/ (accessed September 12, 2018).

12   Bill Hybels, *Courageous Leadership.* (Grand Rapids, Michigan: Zondervan, 2002): 15.

13   Tom Clegg and Warren Bird, *Lost in America: How You and Your Church Can Impact the World Next Door.* (Loveland, Colorado: Group Publishing, 2001): 15.

14   Thom Rainer, *The Unchurched Next Door: Understanding Faith Stages as Keys to Sharing Your Faith.* (Grand Rapids, Michigan: Zondervan,

in our study was that very few of the unchurched population have heard about Christ from a layperson."[15] Failing to share the gospel is a blatant disregard for lost people. This is unacceptable considering many lost people come to Christ through the witness of a friend. Rainer agrees, "The formerly unchurched in our study left little doubt as to the importance of personal evangelism in reaching the unchurched. Over one-half indicated that someone from the church they joined shared Christ with them."[16] God chooses to use every day ordinary people to reach the lost with the gospel of the Lord Jesus and this has been His plan from the beginning of the church. Luke agrees, "When they saw the courage of Peter and John and realized that they were unschooled, ordinary men, they were astonished ..." (Acts 4:13). Personal evangelism is not just for the supposed spiritual elite. Soul winning is for all who call upon the name of the Lord. Failure to engage in personal evangelism is disobedience and this disobedience cripples the mission of the church. Personal evangelism can no longer be neglected if the church is to be faithful in fulfilling the Great Commission (Mt. 28:18-20). Gene Edwards adds, "A revival—a rediscovery—of personal evangelism will, in truth, be the rediscovery of the spirit of New Testament Christianity."[17] This rediscovery is long past due. Soul winning must become a top priority in the local church.

2003): 33.

15 Ibid., 51.

16 Thom Rainer, *Surprising Insights from the Unchurched and Proven Ways to Reach Them.* (Grand Rapids, Michigan: Zondervan, 2001): 43.

17 Gene Edwards, *How to Have a Soul Winning Church.* 14.

The Scope of the Project

While there are many methods of evangelism, they all fall into two primary categories: personal and impersonal. For example, mass evangelism is impersonal. Mass evangelism involves an evangelist and a crowd. The evangelist proclaims the gospel to the multitudes of varying sizes and the crowd listens. Only one person actively participates in the proclamation of the gospel and the others are simply spectators. While this form of evangelism is biblical, necessary, and heartfelt, it is impersonal. The world will not be reached through mass evangelism alone nor did Jesus commission the church to reach the world through mass evangelism. Because of these facts, this project will not address mass evangelism. Instead, it will address the role of personal evangelism in the church—specifically in TFC. This project will seek to identify and measure the attitudes, and actions of the young adult members of TFC concerning personal evangelism.

Personal Evangelism Defined

Personal evangelism must be clearly defined. Mark McCloskey defines it, "At its most foundational level, evangelism is the communication of a message."[18] Personal evangelism is one person sharing a message with another person. Colin Brown adds, "This message is the good news that God has acted for the salvation of the world in the

---

18   Mark McCloskey, *Tell It Often Tell It Well: Making the Most of Witnessing Opportunities.* (San Bernardino, California: Here's Life Publishers, 1985): 17.

incarnation, death, and resurrection of Jesus."[19] Personal evangelism is concisely sharing the message of Jesus who is the Christ. David Watson agrees, "The informative function of personal evangelism is first the telling of the evangel, succinctly and in its essentials, as the reality of God's salvation in the life, death, and resurrection of Jesus Christ."[20] It is clear that personal evangelism is telling the Good News of Jesus, specifically the telling of: His sinless life, His sacrificial death, and His glorious resurrection (1 Cor. 15:2-6). Unfortunately, soul winning, as defined above, appears to be a lost art in the church today. Fewer people are engaged in sharing their faith with non-believers. Gene Edwards writes, "Soul winning has occupied a secondary position in evangelism."[21] This must change. Darrel Robinson adds, "The greatest need of our time is not economic, social, political, or ecological. The greatest need of our generation is for the church to be the church."[22] The greatest need of today's generation is a spiritual one. People need Jesus. The church must step in and meet this need by intentionally equipping and engaging her people to personally share the gospel with their families, neighbors, work associates, and anybody who will listen. Our time is growing shorter. The trumpet call is likely sooner than later. We must act now!

---

19   Colin Brown, *The New International Dictionary of New Testament Theology.* Vol. 2 English Language Translation, (Grand Rapids, Michigan: Zondervan, 1976): 111.

20   David Lowes Watson, "Evangelism: a Disciplinary Approach." *International Bulletin Of Missionary Research* 7, no. 1 (January 1983): 3.

21   Gene Edwards, *How to Have a Soul Winning Church.* 49.

22   Darrell W. Robinson, *Total Church Life.* (Nashville, Tennessee: Broadman & Holman Publishers, 1993): 11.

Misplaced Responsibility

One reason for the lack of zeal for and the lack of participation in personal evangelism is a growing number of those who follow Christ believe the responsibility of evangelism is to be the work of the paid professionals. This misplaced responsibility is detrimental to the mission of the local church. George Godfrey writes, "Satan has deceived multitudes of Christians into believing that the matter of Christian witnessing and soul winning is the responsibility of only full-time workers such as ministers, evangelists, and missionaries."[23] This cannot be farther from the truth. The responsibility of soul winning rests on all believers. When Jesus calls one to follow Him, He invites the same one to engage in personal evangelism (Mt. 4:19). Godfrey continues, "Witnessing for Jesus Christ is part of the normal Christian life."[24] The one who lives for Jesus cannot help but to share about Jesus. Darrel Robinson adds, "… witnessing is the natural expression of the Christian."[25] According to the New Testament following Jesus and sharing the gospel with the lost are mutually inclusive (Acts 1:8). In the early church believers shared their faith regularly even in the face of opposition (Acts 8:4). Yet, there are many today who claim the name of Christ that remain silent. These believers leave the work of evangelism to the paid professionals. Many appear to believe personal evangelism is for the trained church staff only. This simply is not true!

---

23   George Godfrey, *How to Win Souls and Influence People for Heaven*. 16.
24   Ibid., 19.
25   Darrell W. Robinson, *Total Church Life*. 156.

Personal Evangelism is for Everyone

The Bible is abundantly clear the mission of making disciples is to be a church-wide effort (Mt.28:18-20). The words of Jesus clearly record God's plan for the church concerning evangelism and His plan includes His disciples—the church. In the local church today, the membership consists of those who are saved and baptized (Rom. 10:9 and Rom. 6:3). All members are to be ministers and all ministers are to actively participate in making disciples. Bob Russell agrees, "One of the keys to advancing the gospel is for the church to be made up of individuals who consider it their task to do the work of the ministry, rather than having a congregation of people who expect the paid staff to minister to them."[26] In the work of the local church the paid staff are to be the equippers. Russell concurs, "According to the New Testament, the purpose of church leadership is not to do all the work of the church, but to equip the church to minister to one another."[27] This is exactly what the Apostle Paul wrote to the church in Ephesus (Eph. 4:11-12). Warren Wiersbe adds, "The gifted leaders are supposed to equip the saints unto the work of the ministry, unto the building up of the body of Christ."[28] The pastors are to equip the lay people to do the work of the ministry. There are times when lay people do not appropriate this responsibility and pastors step away from their calling to fill in the gaps. Andy Stanley writes, "The moment a

---

26 Bob Russell, *When God Builds a Church 10 Principles for Growing a Dynamic Church*. (West Monroe, Louisiana: Howard Publishing, 2000): 175.

27 Russell, 175.

28 Warren Wiersbe, *Be Rich Gaining The Things That Money Can't Buy*. (Colorado Spring, Colorado: David C. Cook, 1995): 114.

leader steps away from his core competencies, his effectiveness as a leader diminishes. Worse, the effectiveness of every other leader in the organization suffers too."[29] If the church is to thrive in the disciple making effort, which includes personal evangelism, pastors and church staffers must equip their people to do the work of the ministry. This is the biblical model for leadership and the aim of this work specifically in the area of personal evangelism.

The apostle Paul expounds on the ministry of personal evangelism for each church member in his second letter to the church in Corinth (2 Cor. 5:11-21). Paul writes, "We are therefore Christ's ambassadors, as though God were making his appeal through us" (2 Cor. 5:20). The pronoun "we" in the passage indicates that making disciples is the responsibility and privilege of each church member not just the paid staff. Warren Wiersbe agrees, "What a great privilege it is to be heaven's ambassadors to the rebellious sinners of this world!"[30] All believers in the Lord Jesus Christ are called to be His ambassadors. The pastor and his staff must ensure that they are doing all they can with the help of the Holy Spirit to educate, equip, encourage, and empower their people in this manner. This work is designed to help accomplish this at TFC and to offer help for local churches everywhere. The people at TFC will be educated about their role in sharing the gospel and in how to share the gospel. The membership will also be equipped

29 Andy Stanley, *Next Generation Leader Five Essentials for Those Who Will Shape the Future.* (Colorado Springs, Colorado: Multnomah Books, 2003): 21.

30 Warren Wiersbe, *Be Encouraged God Can Turn Your Trials into Triumphs.* (Wheaton, Illinois: Victor Books, 1973): 68.

with the tools to intentionally engage in gospel sharing on a regular basis.

Pastoral Influence

Another reason for this lack of zeal for and the lack of participation in personal evangelism within the church today is there are pastors who are not directly involved in personal evangelism on a regular basis. Johnny Hunt adds, "Pastors are the key to evangelism. If it's not important to them, it will never be important in their churches. Pastors must lead the way."[31] Pastoral influence is important in the area of personal evangelism. Local church pastors should be leading the way. Gene Edwards writes concerning pastors who are leading the way in evangelistic churches, "These men live and breathe, eat and sleep, with just one thought. As they stand in the pulpit, the messages they bring, as they make their announcements, as they plan their church program, as they talk to their people, there is one underlying, unshakeable, unmovable thought; 'We must win souls.'"[32] Soul-winning pastors lead soul-winning churches. Unfortunately, today, this is not the norm across the ecclesiastical landscape of America.

The Early Church

This has not always been the pattern. The early church was active in personal evangelism. There are many examples of personal evangelism recorded in the New Testament (See

---

31   Elrod, Brandon. "Evangelism with Johnny Hunt"-NAMB Podcast. Baptist Press. (Jan 30, 2019).
32   Gene Edwards, *How to Have a Soul Winning Church.* 65.

Appendix B). The early church took Jesus' command to reach the world seriously (Mt. 28:18-20). Luke records the personal evangelistic activities of those in the early church, "Day after day, in the temple courts and from house to house, they never stopped teaching and proclaiming the good news that Jesus is Messiah" (Acts 5:42). In the New Testament personal evangelism is natural and effective. Sharing the gospel is a natural response of those who choose to follow Christ and walk with Him daily. The Gospel writer records the words of Jesus when he calls His first disciples, "Come, follow me, and I will send you out to fish for people" (Mt. 4:19). Answering the Master's call, these men follow Jesus and they fish for men. In the early church, following and fishing are synonymous. There is no distinction between the two. To imagine the possibility of following without fishing is absurd. The same is true of the inverse. Simply stated, those who follow fish and those who fish follow. However, today there are many who claim to know Christ personally through faith in His finished work on the cross and His subsequent resurrection; yet they are not involved in this divine fishing expedition (See Appendix C). This cannot continue. There must be a return to personal evangelism. Thomas Roatch writes, "I believe that for any church or Christian group to be effective in evangelism this group has to be successful in personal evangelism."[33] Christians must personally engage in soul winning. If each Christian would reach one lost person each year the church would double annually and the whole world could be reached in less than a decade.

---

33   Thomas M. Roatch, "Effective Personal Evangelism for Today's Church" Doctoral diss. (Liberty Baptist Theological Seminary, 2011): 1.

The Work of God

A misunderstanding of who is responsible for changing a person's heart is also a reason for the lack of zeal for and the lack of engagement in personal evangelism. The believer must understand that sharing the gospel with a lost person does not always result in salvation; but it does always result in obedience. The apostle Paul writes, "I planted the seed, Apollos watered, but God has been making it grow" (1 Cor. 3:6). While sharing the gospel is the responsibility of the Christian; producing results is the business of God and the work of His Holy Spirit. Gene Edwards adds, "The word 'evangelize' does not denote winning the world to Christ, but presenting the gospel until every man has had an opportunity to decide for or against Christ."[34] According to the Bible, the believer must personally engage in gospel sharing; yet many who call on the name of the Lord never actually engage in personal evangelism. George Barna agrees, "Nearly one-third (31%) believe they should evangelize, but have not done so—at least within the past year."[35] This trend must be reversed. The Word of God compels the Christian to be active in the gospel sharing effort. Jeff Neal and Shonn Keels write, "People must hear the gospel to believe and be saved, and they will not hear unless we tell it often and tell it well."[36] The gospel is powerless if left untold. The church can no longer remain silent. Souls are at stake. The spiritual

34 Gene Edwards, *How to Have a Soul Winning Church.* 55-56.
35 George Barna, "Is Evangelism Going Out of Style?" (2013). http://www.barna.org/barna-update/article/5-barna-update/53-religious-beliefs-vary-widely-by-denomination (accessed September 12, 2018).
36 Jeff J. Neal and Shonn Keels, *Hold the Rope: Having a Heart for the Lost.* (New York City, New York: Morgan and James Publishing, 2013): 28.

condition of men, women, boys, and girls hang in the balance. The Christ follower must share the gospel message often, share it well, and leave the results up to God. God is ultimately the One responsible for changing a person's heart. The believer's responsibility is to simply share the gospel. God's responsibility is to change man's heart. Let the Christian not forget that he is successful every time he shares the gospel.

Prayer and Evangelism

Another reason for this lack of zeal in gospel sharing and for the lack of participation in personal evangelism is the lack of prayer within the church in America today concerning reaching the lost. Corporate prayer is becoming extinct in the church. Leonard Ravenhill agrees, "The prayer meeting is dead or dying."[37] Based on the experience of the author, Ravenhill's assessment of the prayer meeting in the local church appears to be accurate. His assessment is definitely accurate for TFC. This fact is sad considering Christians need God's help in their lives and in their gospel sharing efforts. Leon F. Maurer agrees, "Every Christian needs more power and should earnestly pray that he would meet the Lord's conditions."[38] Prayer cannot be neglected if the believer desires to honor God in his life and in his witness. The prayer ministry at TFC meets every Sunday at 5pm. Typically there are about five people who meet consistently during this time. When these prayer warriors gather, they pray over the prayer requests that are submitted each weekend by the

---

37 Leonard Ravenhill, *Why Revival Tarries.* (Minneapolis, Minnesota: Bethany House, 1987): 21.

38 Leon F. Maurer, *Soul Winning: The Challenge of the Hour.* (Murfreesboro, Tennessee: Sword of the Lord, 1970): 154.

membership via communication cards that are located in the seatback of each chair within the worship center. During the welcome time church members and guests are encouraged to fill out a communication card and submit prayer requests. While there are some who take advantage of this opportunity, few of the requests if any have anything to do with praying for the lost or a lost person. A sample of this prayer list is included in the appendices for your review (See Appendix D). Note that only twenty-six people out of an average attendance of more than six hundred people actually submitted prayer requests on the listed date. There is no significance in the date of this list; however, this list is a valid representation of the number and type of prayer requests submitted each week. The date included is the date of the writing of this piece of the project. Notice only four of the twenty-six people who submitted prayer requests mention a lost person in their request and only two of them specifically ask for prayer concerning a specific lost person's salvation. Please also be assured the names on all of the requests have been changed to protect the anonymity of the individuals who submitted these requests. Also, any confidential requests that were submitted have been omitted as to protect the integrity of the staff of TFC.

It must be noted that about seventy-five people who attend the Wednesday evening meal at TFC also spend a few minutes praying over this same prayer list. The staff at TFC is also faithful at praying over this same list each Tuesday during the weekly staff meeting. Nevertheless, as the prayer list shows, very few prayer requests express any concern for lost people; yet prayer is an essential part of effective personal evangelism efforts. Thomas Roatch agrees, "Prayer, and personal evangelism are inseparable, these two activities work together to accomplish effective evangelism."[39] One must always talk with God about a person before he talks with a person about God. Researcher Thom Rainer adds, "Perhaps more than any other theme, we discovered that the churches successfully reaching the lost focus on the basics: biblical preaching, prayer, intentional witnessing, missions, and comprehensive biblical training in small groups (usually called Sunday School)."[40] Notice prayer is a common denominator among churches that are reaching people through personal evangelism. Prayer and effective evangelism are inseparable. Victor Benavides writes, "Prayer is the asphalt on which we walk to take the gospel of Jesus Christ to the world."[41] Let the American church rise up and pave this road of personal evangelism with prayer. Prayer is exactly what characterized the life and ministry of Jesus and it should characterize the life and ministry of the church too (Mk. 1:35).

Too Busy

The church in some cases is simply too busy to reach people. The smorgasbords of ministries, events, programs, and retreats offered in many churches today often cause the people to lose their focus concerning the mission of the Church—to make disciples. Thom Rainer writes, "Events, activities, and programs outside the process cause people to move in multiple

39   Thomas M. Roatch, "Effective Personal Evangelism for Today's Church" Doctoral diss. (Liberty Baptist Theological Seminary, 2011): 34.

40   Thom Rainer. *Effective Evangelistic Churches.* (Nashville, Tennessee: Broadman and Holman, 1996): 48.

41   Victor H. Benavides, *Inner City Evangelism.* (Alpharetta, Georga: NAMB, 2003): 11.

directions."[42] The busyness causes people to forget why the church exists and leaves them no time to share the gospel with their families, neighbors, friends, and co-workers. The church will do well to slow down, refocus, and build purpose driven ministries that will engage her people in personal evangelism. Sometimes the church must say no to good things in order to say yes to God things. It is possible for a church to be busy about good things and miss what God desires to do in and through her ministry. Often times what is missed in the busyness of the American church is personal evangelism.

The Testimony of the Believer Matters

Another challenge in the church relating to personal evangelism is that Christians all too often look and act no different than non-Christians. Those who claim Christ go to church on the weekends and participate in their religious duties; yet they live as if they do not know Christ. Georg Barna writes, "Believers are largely indistinguishable from non-believers in how they think and live."[43] This lackadaisical approach to the Christian life is diametrically opposed to the advancement of the gospel. The day-to-day testimony of the believer matters. Francis Chan includes in his book the words of Frederick D. Huntington that address this very fact. "It is not scientific doubt, not atheism, not pantheism, not agnosticism, that in our day and in this land is likely to quench the light of the gospel. It is proud, sensuous, selfish, luxurious, church-going,

---

42 Thom Rainer and Eric Geiger, *Simple Church.* (Nashville, Tennessee: Broadman and Holman Publishing, 2006): 77.

43 George Barna, *Growing True Disciples.* (Ventura, California: Issachar Resources, 2000): 14.

hollow-hearted prosperity."[44] Christians everywhere need to repent. Christians must take their eyes off of themselves and place them on Jesus. Only then will personal evangelism take its rightful place in the Church and in the lives of those who make it up. If Christians are not growing in their faith, they are not likely to share the gospel with others. Growing spiritually and personal evangelism are synonymous. Those who are growing in their faith tend to share the gospel regularly. Those who are not growing in their faith tend to remain silent. Gene Edwards writes, "If you are to win a soul to Christ you must put into play the whole Christian life; the Word; prayer; dependence on the Holy Spirit, all the fruits of maturity in Christ."[45] Sharing one's faith typically comes from an overflow of what God is doing in one's life. Those who spend time with Jesus are more likely to tell others about Him. Walking with Jesus and witnessing for Him harmoniously work together.

Invite People to Christ

The lack of zeal for personal evangelism in the church and the lack of active participation in sharing the gospel must be addressed. Many Christians are not regularly involved in personally reaching out to their family, neighbors, work associates, and community members with the gospel of Christ. The attitudes and actions of many in the church concerning soul winning are disappointing at best. Some Christians will invite their friends to church; but rarely invite them to Christ.

---

44 Francis Chan, *Crazy Love*. (Colorado Springs, Colorado: David C. Cook, 2013): 65.

45 Gene Edwards, *How to Have a Soul Winning Church*. 57.

Inviting someone to church is not sharing the gospel. Simply inviting someone to church is not working nor is it a biblical form of evangelism. Gene Edwards writes, "The poorest product on earth to sell a *lost* soul is the church. He could not be less interested."[46] Yet week after week many Christians invite the lost in their circle of influence to church and not to Christ. No wonder many Americans believe that attending church is equal to salvation. This has to change. Christians must invite people to Christ! Inviting people to church is not personal evangelism nor is it working.

The Ministry of the Holy Spirit

A misunderstanding of the ministry of the Holy Spirit in personal evangelism also negatively impacts the zeal for personal evangelism and the lack of participation in the same. John Rice declares, "Winning a soul to trust Christ as Savior is a supernatural business."[47] Winning a soul to trust Christ as Savior involves the work of the Holy Spirit (Jn. 15:26 & 16:8). Lewis Sperry Chafer adds, "The unveiling of the Gospel by the Spirit is necessary and reasonable."[48] This is evident as Jesus promised to give His followers the supernatural power of the Holy Spirit to reach the world with the gospel (Acts 1:8). In the "Great Commission" Jesus promised He would be with His followers until the end of the age as they carried out this

---

46   Ibid., 32.
47   John R. Rice, *The Golden Path to Successful Soul Winning.* (Murfreesboro, Tennessee: The Sword of The Lord Publishers, 1961): 177.
48   Lewis Sperry Chafer, *True Evangelism or Winning Souls by Prayer.* (Findlay, Ohio: Dunham Publishing, 1919): 81.

command to reach the world with the gospel (Mt. 28:20). This abiding presence of the Lord Jesus comes in the person of the Holy Spirit and His presence gives the power necessary for life and personal evangelism. The Holy Spirit fills the Christian with power and direction to be an effective soul winner. Jerry Wiles adds, "In its purest form, soul winning is putting yourself in a position for the Holy Spirit to win souls through what He prompts you to say and do."[49] The soul winner is an instrument in the hands of Almighty God. While God uses the believer in the process of winning souls, it is the work of the Holy Spirit that changes a lost person's heart. John Rice explains, "The power of the Holy Spirit is required in witnessing, for He alone can bring conviction, repentance, and new birth."[50] Rice's explanation is in harmony with Jesus' words concerning the ministry of the Holy Spirit recorded in the Gospel of John (16:8-11). Lewis Sperry Chafer adds, "The Spirit thus also enlightens the darkened mind concerning the complete and sufficient judgment of all sin in the cross of Christ."[51] The soul winner's responsibility is to be obedient. The Christian is to simply share the gospel. The Holy Spirit is the One who will convict the sinner of his sin as the cross of the Lord Jesus is lifted high through the telling of the gospel. In this beautiful exchange, the apostle Paul reminds the church that God is ultimately the One who changes the heart of the lost person (1 Cor. 3:6). Personal evangelism is a partnership. The Christian is the one who proclaims the gospel, and God is the One who changes lives.

---

49 Jerry Wiles, *How to Win Others to Christ Your Personal, Practical Guide to Evangelism.* (Nashville, Tennessee: Thomas Nelson, 1992): 5.

50 John R. Rice, *The Golden Path to Successful Soul Winning.* 177.

51 Lewis Sperry Chafer, *True Evangelism or Winning Souls by Prayer.* 67.

Salvation is a Process

While salvation is an event, a time when one surrenders to the Lord Jesus and is saved (Rom. 10:9), it is also a process (1 Cor. 3:6). This process of salvation starts with God even before time began, "He has saved us and called us to a holy life—not because of anything we have done but because of his own purpose and grace. This grace was given us in Christ Jesus before the beginning of time, but it has now been revealed through the appearing of our Savior, Christ, Jesus, who has destroyed death and has brought life and immortality to light through the gospel" (2 Tim. 2:9-10). Those who come to salvation in Christ have been known from eternity past, "All of the inhabitants of the earth will worship the beast—all whose names have not been written in the Lamb's book of life, the Lamb who was slain from the creation of the world" (Rev. 13:8). Salvation is made possible because of the obedience of the Son of God (Phil. 2:6-8). As the process continues God draws the lost sinner (Jn. 6:44). This drawing may be the result of natural revelation and/or divine revelation (Rom. 1:18-20 & 10:17). At some point in the process of salvation God will use the gospel message (Rom. 1:16 & Eph. 1:13-15). As the gospel message is presented, the Holy Spirit gives testimony to the Truth and God changes a life for all of eternity (Jn. 15:26). God uses people to present the gospel message (Rom. 10:14-15). Therefore, the Christian must yield to the leading of the Holy Spirit and share the gospel with the lost in his circle of influence. Neal and Keels write, "The proclamation of the gospel is powerful and necessary for getting people close to Jesus!"[52] The process of salvation requires the

---

52   Jeff J. Neal and Shonn Keels, *Hold the Rope.* 102.

telling of the gospel. For the gospel is powerless to accomplish its purpose until it is told.

God's Power

The Christian must rely on the Holy Spirit in his gospel sharing efforts. Leonard Ravenhill writes, "Today God is bypassing men—not because they are too ignorant, but because they are too self-sufficient."[53] The believer who desires to win souls cannot neglect to call upon the Lord and yield to His direction. The effective soul winner will be faithful to call upon the Lord and yield to the leading of the Holy Spirit in his life and in his gospel sharing efforts. The church must recognize and depend on the power and presence of the Holy Spirit to be effective in personal evangelism. The Holy Spirit will lead the soul winner if he will simply ask for direction and yield in response (James 1:5). John Rice adds, "To ask God for special leading in soul winning is only doing in particular what is everywhere commanded and taught in the Bible."[54] A great illustration of the need for the soul winner to depend on the leading of the Holy Spirit in personal evangelism is recorded in the book of Acts where the Holy Spirit clearly spoke to both Cornelius (the recipient of the gospel) and Peter (the gospel deliverer) during their times of prayer (10:1-23). Each of these men prayed and God responded. Each of these men yielded to the leading of Holy Spirit's direction and salvation was the result. The church in America will do well to take note of this illustration and to practice the same.

---

53   Leonard Ravenhill, *Why Revival Tarries*. 39.
54   John R. Rice, *The Golden Pathway to Successful Soul Winning*. 179.

The Process Takes Time

Inviting people to Christ is most often like a marathon not a sprint. Sharing the gospel effectively typically takes time and it unfolds best through growing relationships. In these relationships, trust is built, and trust is key in earning the right to share the gospel. Jeff Neal and Shonn Keels write, "Relationships are key and fundamental in sharing the gospel. If we desire to influence the world with the gospel, we must build relationships with people who are far from God."[55] People are more likely to respond to the gospel because of the witness of God's work in a friend's life. Tom Clegg and Warren Bird agree, "Your church—beginning with you—must change its heart and behavior, learning to build intentional relationships with people who aren't yet Christians."[56] The lost want to see that Jesus is real before they make a choice to follow Him. Alvin Reid adds, "Skills, methods, and experience in evangelism are good; doctrine is essential. But the gospel presented by a believer whose life exemplifies the character of Christ is best."[57] Christianity is something that is caught as much as it is taught. A life well lived will surely earn the right to be heard by a lost friend. A growing challenge is that many Christians look no different than the lost around them. Charles Kelley, the president of New Orleans Baptist Seminary says, "Our problem is that

---

55 Jeff J. Neal and Shonn Keels, *Hold the Rope: Having a Heart for the Lost.* 9.

56 Tom Clegg and Warren Bird, *Lost in America: How You and Your Church Can Impact the World Next Door.* (Loveland, Colorado: Group Publishing, 2001): 21.

57 Alvin Reid, *Evangelism Handbook: Biblical, Spiritual, Intentional, Missional.* (Nashville Tennessee: B&H Academic, 2009): 198.

more of us do not look and live like Jesus."[58] Vance Havner adds, "Most church members live so far below the standard, you would have to backslide to be in fellowship with them."[59] Lazy and lukewarm living hurt the church and stifle personal evangelism. Lost people are looking for something to believe in and someone to lead them to this belief. This someone will inevitably be the one whose life looks like Jesus. Christians must pray, commit to a lifestyle of holy living, and share the gospel when given the opportunity. Unfortunately, this is not common in the church today.

58   Michael Catt, "Dr. Chuck Kelley—Southern Baptists Are the New Methodists." October 10, 2012. Accessed September 26, 2018.

59   Vance Havner, "Vance Havner Quotes." Freedom Christian Quotes.

CHAPTER ONE

The Challenge

T he challenge at The First Church (TFC) is the majority of the membership is not actively engaged in personal evangelism. While TFC is a great church, she is living in disobedience to the clarion call of Jesus to reach the world with the gospel. Souls are at stake. The difference is heaven or hell. The church must wake up and answer the call of Christ. TFC is made up of loving people, and there are many great things going on in this church. The music is God honoring, the preaching is Christ exalting, and the people genuinely love God and others. They are known in their city as a very hospitable church. However, there remains a major challenge. As mentioned, the challenge is the majority of the membership at TFC is not consistently sharing the gospel with the lost in her community. The purpose of this project is to specifically examine the young adults at TFC with particular reference to their lack of attention to and engagement in personal evangelism in order to develop a church-wide personal evangelism training ministry to be sponsored, led, and conducted by the project director. This challenge is not unique to TFC. There are churches all over America that are struggling to get their people to engage in personal evangelism.

It appears the attitude of many at TFC is that personal evangelism should be left up to the paid professionals. This conviction is both unfair and unbiblical. John Mark Terry writes, "A pastor, or even a pastor and staff, cannot reach the church community for Christ. Many church members try to place the responsibility for outreach on the pastor alone, but this is unbiblical and impractical."[60] While this is unacceptable, personal evangelism has unofficially been assigned to the senior pastor and the pastoral staff. However, most of the evangelism from the senior pastor and his staff comes by way of mass evangelism: either from the platform, camps, retreats, and/or special mass evangelism efforts. This approach leaves personal evangelism virtually non-existent among the staff and the membership. The lack of personal interaction with the lost concerning the gospel message is not only disappointing it is antithetical to the example of Jesus in the Scripture. Jesus clearly sets the example of how to make personal evangelism a priority. Consider a few examples.

Jesus and the Samaritan Woman

Jesus often speaks to the multitudes—mass evangelism; but not at the expense of personally interacting with the lost.

---

60   John Mark Terry, *Church Evangelism: Basic Principles, Diverse Models.* (Nashville, Tennessee: B&H Academic, 1997): 73.

Relationships matter to Jesus as He carries out His earthly ministry. Consider the woman at the well recorded in the fourth chapter of John. J. Dwight Pentecost notes, "Concerning the journey of Jesus from Judea to Galilee, John stated that He "had to go through Samaria" (John 4:4). The word "had" implies necessity."[61] The journey through Samaria is by divine design. Pentecost continues, "… it seems as though the necessity arose out of Christ's understanding of God's will for Him."[62] By traveling through Samaria, Jesus crosses many barriers: color, culture, and creed to position Himself in the presence of one who is searching for a relationship with God. Led by the Holy Spirit, Jesus breaks the traditions of the Jews to go through Samaria to fulfill His purpose on earth, "…just as the Son of Man did not come to be served, but to serve, and to give his life as a ransom for many" (Mt. 20:28). Jesus came to earth to sacrifice His life for the sins of the Samaritan woman and the sin of the world (Jn. 3:16). Jesus personally delivers this message to her as she inquires about the coming of the Messiah. "The woman said, 'I know that the Messiah' (called Christ) 'is coming. When he comes, he will explain everything to us.' Then Jesus declared, 'I, the one speaking to you—I am he'" (Jn. 4:25-26). Jesus personally shares the message of Christ—the gospel with the Samaritan woman—a lost person. Personal evangelism is His normal practice.

Jesus Calls Matthew

The calling of Matthew is another great example of the personal nature of evangelism in the life and ministry of Jesus.

61   J. Dwight Pentecost, *The Words and Works of Jesus Christ*. (Grand Rapids, Michigan: Zondervan, 1981): 131.

62   Ibid., 131.

The calling of Matthew also demonstrates the great lengths that Jesus takes to reach a lost person (Mt. 9:9-13). Jesus again breaks the customs of the religious leaders of His day and goes to the house of a sinner to interact with more sinners. Pentecost points out, "The righteous Jews of the community would not have responded to an invitation to come to the house of a tax collector; so the banquet was filled with fellow tax collectors and others who fell into the category of sinners. Jesus did not draw back from association with such people."[63] The practice of Jesus is to penetrate the lost culture around Him. Matthew records, "When the Pharisees saw this, they asked his disciples, 'Why does your teacher eat with tax collectors and sinners?'" (9:11). The reason Jesus eats with tax collectors and sinners is simple—building relationships with the lost matters to Jesus. Jesus says, "For I have not come to call the righteous, but sinners" (9:13). If building relationships with sinners and personally reaching lost people is important to Jesus, the church must make personal evangelism a priority.

Jesus Visits Zacchaeus

The Gospel of Luke chapter nineteen records another personal evangelism encounter of Jesus with Zacchaeus a sinful "chief tax collector" who was ostracized by his own people (19:1-10). J. Dwight Pentecost adds, "Christ chose to spend the night in the home of this despised tax collector."[64] In this encounter, as was Jesus' custom, Jesus breaks the traditions of the religious

---

63   Ibid., 155.
64   Ibid., 366.

Jews and personally meets with a sinner—Zacchaeus. Luke writes, "When Jesus reached the spot, he looked up and said to him, 'Zacchaeus, come down immediately. I must stay at your house today'" (19:5). Personally, meeting with Zacchaeus is a priority for Jesus, "For the Son of Man came to seek and to save the lost" (19:10). The personal nature of evangelism cannot be neglected if the church studies and seeks to imitate the life and ministry of Jesus. The Scriptures and the testimony of the Savior demand the church increase the priority she places on personal evangelism.

Relationships Matter Most to the Master

The above three personal examples of Jesus demonstrate the importance that He places on relationships. The importance Jesus places on relationships is consistent in both His life and His teachings (Mt. 22:34-40). An expert in the law once asked Jesus, "Teacher, which is the greatest commandment in the Law?" (Mt. 22:36). Jesus' response places a high priority on relationships. First, Jesus' response places the highest value on one's relationship with God. Matthew writes, "Jesus replied: 'Love the Lord your God with all your heart and with all your soul and with all your mind.' This is the first and greatest commandment" (22:37-38). Second, Jesus' response places an equally high value on one's relationship with others. Matthew continues, "And the second is like it: 'Love your neighbor as yourself'" (22:39). Jesus is clear, relationships matter most to God and relationships must be governed by love. Frank Stagg agrees, "The key word in the **great commandment** as well as the **second** that is like it, is **love**"[65] (original author's emphasis). Love fulfills the laws of God. Matthew writes, "All the Law and the Prophets hang on these two commandments" (22:40). Loving God and loving one's neighbor are to be top priorities in the life of a Christian. Loving God and loving one's neighbor are impossible apart from a life devoted to the practice of personal evangelism. Jesus said, "If you love me, keep my commands" (Jn. 14:15). Loving God is obeying Him. Loving God is serving Him. Loving God is sharing Him with others.

Busy and Distracted

Unfortunately, many at TFC are not personally sharing Christ with others. Sadly, many of the members do not recognize their lack of zeal for personal evangelism and their lack of participation in the same because they are too busy and distracted. The evangelical delirium of the membership may also stem from the fact that the church is experiencing substantial growth. The growth at TFC itself is exciting, however much of the growth is not by way of salvations. The church records reveal that most of the growth is from transferred memberships (See Appendix A). The transfer to baptism ratio from 2013 to 2018 is 3:1. There are three transfers per every salvation. The ratio is not concerning on the surface. However, a deeper study of the statistics reveals most of the salvations over these six years are from the youth and children's ministries and these salvations are a direct result of mass evangelism—summer camps. Most of

---

65   Frank Stagg and Henry E. Turlington, *The Broadman Bible Commentary: Matthew–Mark.* (Nashville, Tennessee: Broadman Press, 1969): 209.

these salvations are not a direct result of personal evangelism. As earlier mentioned, mass evangelism is biblical and necessary; but it cannot be the sole source of evangelism for a local church. Leon Maurer writes, "The Holy Spirit was not only given for power to reach the masses, but also to reach individuals."[66] TFC must equip and engage her members in personal evangelism. Reaching the world through personal evangelism is what Jesus commissioned the church to do. Sharing the gospel with the lost is also what Jesus prayed His followers would do just before He ascended into Heaven.

Jesus Prays for Personal Evangelism

Jesus not only commissions His disciples to be soul winners. He also prays for them to strategically make the gospel known to all nations. This prayer is not done in solace away from His disciples. Jesus prays among them illustrating the importance of the content of His prayer. J. Dwight Pentecost notes, "In His prayer in their hearing, He had said that He was sending them into the world for the same purpose that the Father had sent Him into the world (John 17:18); namely, to make the Father known."[67] This is a significant moment. Those who follow Jesus will represent Him to the world. The apostle Paul writes, "We are therefore Christ's ambassadors, as though God were making his appeal through us" (2 Cor. 5:20). God is choosing to reach the world through His people. This is phenomenal. God being both omniscient and omnipotent chooses to use His people to

---

66   Leon F. Maurer, *Soul Winning: The Challenge of the Hour.*
     (Murfreesboro, Tennessee: Sword of the Lord, 1970): 147.
67   J. Dwight Pentecost, *The Words and Works of Jesus Christ.* 509.

reach the world. He did not choose a certain type of worship service, a special method of evangelism, an angelic being, the expanse of the skies; nor did He choose a certain style of music. No, God clearly chooses His people to accomplish His global purpose of making disciples of all nations. The church must never forget the purpose of God for His people. The church must also stop neglecting the purpose of God for His people. Christians must actively engage in the soul-winning effort.

The Current Context of The First Church

Currently, there are a few churches in this midwestern city experiencing turnover in senior leadership due to retirements and other various reasons. As a result, many individuals from these churches have made their way to TFC. Nevertheless, there is no systematic plan to equip people for personal evangelism and to employ them to do the same. The lack of such a plan goes unnoticed, as the people of TFC appear to be content. This must change if TFC is to maximize her redemptive potential as a local church. Alphonse Turner writes, "The local church plays a critical role in evangelism, for it is the force that is most capable and strategically positioned to reach the unchurched."[68] The church indeed is the force that Jesus sent the Holy Spirit to empower for such a task—global evangelization (Acts 1:8). The need for the church to rise up is ever increasing. George Barna reports, "The adult population in the United States has grown by 15 percent. During that same period, the number of adults who do not attend church has nearly doubled, rising from 39

---

68   Alphonse Turner Jr, "A Personal Evangelism Training Plan" Doctoral
       diss. Temple Baptist Seminary, Fayetteville, North Carolina, 2013, 3.

million to 75 million—a 92 percent increase!"[69] However, many Christians are not aware of how many people in their own communities do not know Jesus. Thom Rainer agrees, "Many Christians do not realize how unevangelized and unchurched America has become."[70] Year after year the church in America continues to lose influence and size in the United States. John Dickerson adds, "By multiple accounts, evangelical believers are between 7 and 9 percent of the United States population."[71] The church in America has grown smaller and smaller. It is time to reverse this trend.

TFC is strategically located in a midwestern city in the United States. TFC moved to her current location more than a decade ago anticipating an explosion of growth in this area of the city. The move proved to be a smart decision. As anticipated, the area exploded in growth and the church was one of the largest in the region. However, these fruitful times were followed by some dark years and a severe decline in membership. The church dropped from averaging over 2,000 to 200 in Sunday school attendance. In 2011, the current senior pastor who was the youth pastor back when the church was a true beacon of hope in this growing midwestern city was called to lead the church out of the valley. At the time, TFC was running around 300 in Sunday school attendance. Since the installment of his

69 George Barna, "Number of Unchurched Adults Has Nearly Doubled Since 1991." *Barna Group*, May 4, 2004. http://barna.org (accessed September 26, 2018).

70 Thom Rainer, *Surprising Insights from the Unchurched and Proven Ways to Reach Them*. 33.

71 John S. Dickerson, *The Great Evangelical Recession 6 Factors That Will Crash the American Church … and How to Prepare*. (Grand Rapids, Michigan: BakerBooks, 2013): 26.

pastorate, the church has doubled in Sunday school attendance; yet as explained earlier there is no real passion for soul winning among the membership. During this time there has also been a noticeable trend of declining numbers in Sunday evening discipleship. The decline is so substantial that Sunday evening discipleship no longer exists. The conviction of the author is that somehow the two are related. Jim Austin agrees, "You cannot divorce evangelism and discipleship."[72] People who are deeply committed to the study of the Word of God are also committed to the work of God. George Barna writes, "When individuals are single-minded in their devotion to God, their commitment to His ways and His principles becomes much deeper, much more intense."[73] The greater commitment to God's Word will result in a greater commitment to His work. George Barna adds, "They will gladly share their faith in Christ with non-believers because they understand their responsibility to other people and to God, because they simply cannot contain their own excitement about the privilege of relating to God."[74] Learning God's Word and living God's Word are one and the same. Christians who are active in the study of the Bible are typically active in living it out as well. Growing in relationship with Jesus will feed one's desire to reach people with the gospel of the Lord Jesus. Growing people reach people. Evangelism will be a natural overflow of an active intentional walk with the Lord. Luke agrees, "When they saw the courage of Peter and

---

72 Jim Austin, Staff Workshop at TFC with Dr. Jim Austin, (a Midwestern City: September 23, 2019).

73 George Barna, *Growing True Disciples*. (Ventura, California: Issachar Resources, 2000): 8.

74 Ibid., 9.

John and realized they were unschooled, ordinary men, they were astonished, and they took note that these men had been with Jesus" (Acts 4:13). A close walk with Jesus is the key to Peter and John's newly found courage to evangelize the very people who could persecute them even to death for proclaiming the gospel. Similarly, today, those who have "been with Jesus" cannot go long without sharing their faith.

The Example of the Early Disciples

Consider John's account of the calling of Jesus' first disciples. J. Dwight Pentecost writes, "John had publicly identified Jesus as the Messiah to the nation Israel."[75] John sees Jesus and proclaims, "Look, the Lamb of God, who takes away the sin of the world" (Jn. 1:29)! On the next day John sees Jesus and repeats the declaration that Jesus is the "Lamb of God" (Jn. 1:36). John's disciples understood this to be the fulfillment of the promise God made concerning the Messiah. Andrew now understood this too. Pentecost continues, "After the day spent with Jesus, Andrew was convinced beyond all doubt that He was what John had proclaimed Him to be, the Messiah."[76] Upon having received this knowledge and walking with Jesus Andrew immediately gives his new faith away. The Bible records, "The first thing Andrew did was to find his brother Simon and tell him, 'We have found the Messiah' (that is, the Christ.) And he brought him to Jesus" (Jn. 1:41-42). Knowing and walking with Jesus compels Andrew to share the gospel with his brother. An authentic relationship with Christ is contagious. Those who

---

75   J. Dwight Pentecost, 111.
76   Ibid., 112.

experience Christ and walk intimately with Him are driven to share their experience with others.

John's account of the calling of the first disciples continues with Jesus' personal call of Philip, "Follow me" (1:44). William E. Hull writes, "It defines discipleship in relational rather than in intellectual, emotional, or actional terms."[77] Jesus invited Philip to follow Him as a person. Hull continues, "Philip was not offered an idea to ponder, a mood to experience, or a task to accomplish, but a person to obey."[78] Philip's call was about relationship. Philip hears John's message concerning the Lamb of God, experiences Jesus, and decides to follow Him. After experiencing Jesus and choosing to follow Him, "Philip found Nathanael and told him, 'We have found the one Moses wrote about in the Law, and about whom the prophets also wrote— Jesus of Nazareth, the son of Joseph'" (Jn. 1:45). Philip, like Andrew, walks with Jesus and has to tell someone about his Savior. J. Dwight Pentecost agrees, "Like Andrew before him, Philip reached out to bear witness of Christ's person …".[79] Philip is compelled to share with Nathanael what he has discovered—a relationship with the Messiah. Philip cannot keep silent. The church must learn from these examples and imitate the personal evangelism habits of Jesus and the early disciples. The church must give away her faith as often as possible.

Interestingly enough Jesus' final words to His disciples resemble the first words He used to call His disciples. Jesus says

---

77   Malcolm O. Tolbert and William E. Hull, *The Broadman Bible Commentary: Luke—John.* (Nashville, Tennessee: Broadman Press, 1970): 225.

78   Ibid., 225.

79   J. Dwight Pentecost, 112.

to His first disciples—two fishermen, "Come follow me, and I will send you out to fish for people" (Mt. 4:19). His first and final words in relationship to the followership of His disciples are the same. Jesus calls and commissions His followers to reach people with the Good News of salvation (Mt. 28:18-20). It could not be any clearer. Charles Spurgeon writes, "Soul winning is the chief business of the Christian minister; indeed, it should be the main pursuit of every true believer."[80] Those who follow Christ are called and commissioned to engage in the gospel-sharing crusade. However, all believers must also be aware they face a real enemy in this gospel-sharing crusade. This enemy should not be taken lightly. The apostle Peter warns, "Your enemy the devil prowls around like a roaring lion looking for someone to devour" (1 Pet. 5:8).

The Enemy is at Work

The ancient enemy of God's people is lurking around working diligently to destroy the redemptive work of the church. The apostle Peter writes, "Be alert and of sober mind. Your enemy the devil prowls around like a roaring lion looking for someone to devour" (1 Peter 5:8). God's people face a real enemy. Merrill Unger agrees, "The whole history of the world subsequent to Christ is a struggle against the empire of Satan."[81] Satan, the ancient serpent has been working throughout history to thwart the plan of God to relate to His most prized possession—people. After having disobeyed God in the Garden of Eden, Eve was

---

80   Charles Spurgeon, *The Soul Winner*. (Louisville, Kentucky: GLH Publishing, 2015): 2.

81   Merrill F. Unger, *Unger's Bible Dictionary*. (Chicago, Illinois: Moody Press, 1985): 973.

asked by God what she had done. The Bible records her response, "The woman said, 'The serpent deceived me, and I ate'" (Gen. 3:14). Satan is the master deceiver. Satan deceived Eve in the Garden and he still works overtime to deceive the church today. Satan regularly attempts to lull the church to sleep concerning her responsibility of reaching people. The apostle Paul adds, "… Satan himself masquerades as an angel of light" (2 Cor. 11:14). Satan, as an angel of light, desires to stand in the way of God's redemptive work. The deception of the devil comes in many forms and most of these forms are attractive. Believers must be wise and remain vigilant in prayer in order not to fall prey to Satan's schemes. The devil also works to blind the lost from seeing the Truth. Paul writes, "The god of this age has blinded the minds of unbelievers, so that they cannot see the light of the gospel that displays the glory of Christ, who is the image of God" (2 Cor. 4:4). Believers must not get discouraged. Emil Brunner writes, "The most important truth about the Devil is this: Jesus Christ has conquered him."[82] Jesus is victorious, and He is the light of the world. G.R. Beasley-Murray agrees, "The devil belongs to darkness, but the gospel opens men to the light of God."[83] The church must be faithful to share the gospel light. The church must also remember that the greatest weapons against this blinding work of Satan are prayer, the Holy Spirit, and God's Word. The apostle Paul illustrates this in his life and ministry.

---

82 Emil Brunner, *The Christian Doctrine of Creation and Redemption*. (London: Lutterworth, 1952): 145.

83 G.R. Beasley-Murray, *The Broadman Bible Commentary: Luke—John*. (Nashville, Tennessee: Broadman Press, 1971): 28.

The Example of the Apostle Paul

The apostle Paul spends three weeks in Thessalonica and plants a thriving church (Acts 17:1-9). Later in a response to a report received from this new church Paul writes, "For we know, brothers and sisters loved by God, that he has chosen you, because our gospel came to you not simply with words but also with power, with the Holy Spirit and deep conviction" (1 Thess. 1:4-5). Paul emphasizes the weapons he used to take the gospel to Thessalonica—prayer, the Holy Spirit, and God's Word. As mentioned in the introduction to this paper, prayer is often taken for granted in the church. Many Christians use prayer as a last resort when prayer should be the first response for all believers. In personal evangelism, prayer is the channel in which one receives the power of the Holy Spirit for an effective gospel witness. Lewis Sperry Chafer agrees, "All evangelism must begin with prayer."[84] Leon Maurer adds, "There is no such thing as a Christian doing the complete will of God and His work without His power; otherwise, the work is done in the energy of the flesh."[85] Prayer and the power of the Holy Spirit work together. Paul also writes that his message sprang from deep conviction. Herschel Hobbs notes, "The apostle and his aides had full assurance that in the Holy Spirit the gospel was a transforming power."[86] This deep conviction was a result of the Word of God being active and alive in Paul's life. Paul believed God's Word and had personally experienced the transforming

---

84   Lewis Sperry Chafer, *True Evangelism or Winning Souls by Prayer.* 88.

85   Leon F. Maurer, *Soul Winning: The Challenge of the Hour.* 154.

86   Herschel H. Hobbs, *The Broadman Bible Commentary: 2 Corinthians—Philemon.* (Nashville, Tennessee: Broadman Press, 1971): 267.

power of the Holy Spirit in his own life. The more one spends time reading and studying God's Word the more effective he will be in his witness to others (Josh. 1:8).

Effective personal evangelism is not possible apart from the work of the Holy Spirit and the Word of God being made alive in the life of a believer. The membership of TFC must learn from the example of Paul, lean into the ministry of personal evangelism, and be faithful in the battle for souls. There is too much at stake for TFC to sit back and rest in the glory of her past and the fruit of the transferred growth of today. Change must occur or the damage that will be done will be eternal in its consequences. This church must return to the pattern of ministry set forth in the New Testament—personal evangelism. Lives are at stake and eternity hangs in the balance.

The Impact of Post-Christian America

The world around the American church is rapidly changing. Perhaps the world is changing faster today than in times past. John Dickerson writes, "… culture is changing faster than it typically has in world history."[87] This change creates an even greater problem for the church to engage in personal evangelism in a post-Christian America. People are not as open as they once were to hear the gospel. George Barna agrees, "It's not easy to be the kind of Christian that Jesus longs to have as His ambassadors in this place, at this time."[88] The general population is growing colder to gospel influence and

---

87   John S. Dickerson, *The Great Evangelical Recession*. 42.
88   George Barna, *Futurcast*. (Carol Stream, Illinois: BarnaBooks, 2011): x.

even antagonistic toward Christianity. John Dickerson warns, "The culture is not just apathetically drifting from Christianity, as it did in the late 20th century. Now its leading edges are violently reacting to the grip that conservative Christianity and the religious right held for so many decades." [89] A return to personal evangelism is imperative. Relationships will be key in winning people to Christ as the culture becomes increasingly pagan. The church must be intentional in building relationships with the lost. If TFC does not correct this challenge—lack of participation in personal evangelism, divine discipline is a possibility. If TFC continues to neglect personal evangelism, the church will likely face consequences for her disobedience. One of these consequences is the attendance patterns will begin to drop. Nationally attendance in churches is already in a downward spiral. Barry Kosmin and Ariela Keyser agree "As a percentage of the population, evangelicalism is shrinking in the United States." [90] If the challenge is not corrected at TFC the budget will likely suffer. In the U.S. decreasing budgets and cutting staff is already the norm. The oldest most generous generation alive today makes up more than half of the church in America. John Dickerson warns, "Over the next twelve years, this faithful and reliable generation will pass away. As they do, total giving will decrease by as much as half for typical evangelical ministries—nationally, regionally, and locally." [91]

---

89 John S. Dickerson, *The Great Evangelical Recession.* 46.

90 Barry Kosmin and Ariela Keyser, *"2009 American Religious Identification Survey, Summary."* (Hartford, Connecticut: Trinity College, 2009): 17.

91 John S. Dickerson, *The Great Evangelical Recession 6 Factors That Will Crash … the American Church … and How to Prepare.* 82.

When giving decreases the elimination of key staff members is inevitable. And the giving at TFC will begin to decrease with the older generation dying off. The author of this work observed in his research that there have been more funerals in the last six years at TFC than he personally experienced in his first twenty years of ministry. As the budget decreases, there will also be less money to do ministry. The impact of the church on her city will wane. It is time for the church to wake up and return to the ministry of personally reaching people. TFC must make personal evangelism a priority.

Please remember, while this doctoral ministry project is designed to identify and address the challenge at TFC, the challenge identified and addressed is not unique to this church. The American evangelical church as a whole is failing in the issue at hand. According to recent research, very few who claim Christ are personally sharing their faith on a consistent basis and many of them are not sharing Christ at all. However, there is hope. This trend can be reversed! If the downward trend is to be reversed, you and I must take personal evangelism and the training of the same seriously. We must *Go Fish* and lead our churches to do the same!

CHAPTER TWO

THE PLAN TO
ADDRESS THE CHALLENGE

The Scripture clearly addresses the challenge discovered at
The First Church (TFC). As earlier stated, the challenge at
TFC is the majority of the membership is not actively engaged
in personally sharing the gospel of the Lord Jesus Christ. In
short, the church is growing in disobedience to the clarion call
of the Lord Jesus to reach the world with the gospel. The plan to
address the problem is supported with both biblical teachings
and current literature. The purpose of this project is to examine
the young adults at TFC with particular reference to their
lack of attention to and engagement in personal evangelism in
order to develop a church-wide personal evangelism-training
ministry. The project is designed to properly disciple the young
adults at TFC and to engage them in a lifestyle committed to
personal evangelism. It is the conviction of this author that the
project will be implemented for years to come with the end
goal of properly discipling the entire membership in personal
evangelism and engaging them in a lifestyle committed to

the same. This chapter contains a review of a few key biblical passages and current literature that support the plan for this doctoral ministry project--dissertation. This chapter also includes a step-by-step plan to address the challenge at TFC. Understanding that the challenge at TFC is not an isolated one, the plan to address the problem is designed with other churches in mind. The plan is designed to be easily duplicated in any church in America and around the world.

The Bible is Abundantly Clear

The biblical mandate to evangelize the world is clear (Mk. 16:15). There is no confusion in the words of the Lord Jesus often referred to as the "Great Commission." The word of the Lord concerning personal evangelism is a clarion call for all who claim Christ. These marching orders of the Lord Jesus are given on a couple of occasions. Alfred Edersheim notes, "... this twofold testimony comes to us from St. Matthew and St. Mark."[92] At the end of Jesus' earthly ministry Matthew records His message, "All authority in heaven and on earth has been given to me. Therefore, go and make disciples of all nations, baptizing them in the name of the Father and of the Son and of the Holy Spirit, and teaching them to obey everything I have commanded you. And surely, I am with you always, to the very end of the age" (Mt. 28:18-20). Bill Jones adds, "At this same rendezvous Jesus most likely makes the statement found in Mark 16:15, 'Go into all the world and preach the gospel to all creation.' Putting these two verses together, we could say that

---

92   Alfred Edersheim, *The Life and Times of Jesus the* Messiah. (Grand Rapids, Michigan: Wm. B. Eerdmans Publishing, 1972): 651.

we as followers of Christ must go to every people group in the world and explain to each person in that group how they can have a personal relationship with God through faith in the Lord Jesus Christ."[93] Let there be no ambiguity concerning the Lord's call. His words are clear, and His message is for all who claim His name. The church is to proclaim the message of the gospel to all nations. Believers must tell it often and tell it well. Soul winning must be the chief aim of the church and those who make it up. This is a huge responsibility and it also is a great privilege. The commission of Jesus is a biblical motivation for this project.

The Clarion Call of Christ

The call of Jesus is another biblical motivation for this project. As earlier mentioned, Jesus calls His followers to become "fishers of men" (Mt. 4:19). Interestingly in the calling of His disciples, Jesus does not say His followers should become fishers of men or they could become fishers of men. No, Jesus clearly says, "Follow me and I will make you fishers of men" (Mt. 4:19). The call of Jesus is clear His disciples will be fishers of men. Those who choose to follow Jesus will share the gospel with people who are far from God. Afterall, following is fishing, and fishing is following!

The Cry of the Lost

The cry of the lost is another biblical motivation for this project (Acts 16:30). Luke records the event when Paul and

---

93   Bill Jones, *Putting Together the Puzzle of the New Testament.* (Colorado Springs, Colorado: Biblica Publishing, 2009): 119.

Silas were traveling together and sharing the gospel whenever possible. After Paul casts an evil spirit out of a slave girl who could tell the future, he and Silas are placed in a Roman jail. While in Jail, Paul and Silas sing hymns and give praise to God. As they are praising the Lord and singing to Him, a violent earthquake shakes the place, and the jail doors are opened. When the jailer wakes up and notices the prison doors have opened and the men are no longer in chains, he draws his sword to kill himself. Paul, not wanting the man to die without Christ, shouted, "Don't harm yourself! We are all here" (Acts 16:28)! In response to the testimony of these men who loved the Lord Jesus, the jailer cries out, "Sirs, what must I do to be saved?" (Acts 16:30). This cry of the lost is a resounding cry in this post-Christian world. Many do not even know they are crying; but if the church will listen with spiritual ears the cry of the lost is ringing loudly and clearly. Jeff Neal and Shonn Keels write, "The greatest need in all the world is to be loved."[94] People are spiritually empty and looking for love in all the wrong places. The church has the answer, and His name is Jesus.

Heavenly Accountability

The judgment seat of Christ is another biblical motivation for this project (2 Cor. 5:6-11). The apostle Paul writes, "Therefore we are always confident and know that as long as we are at home in the body we are away from the Lord. For we

---

94   Jeff J. Neal and Shonn Keels, *Hold the Rope Having A Heart for the Lost,* (New York City, New York: Morgan and James Publishing, 2013): 24.

live by faith, not by sight. We are confident, I say, and would prefer to be away from the body and at home with the Lord" (6-9). Paul teaches, it is better to be with the Lord; but there is a season where man must live on earth. He continues, "So we make it our goal to please him, whether we are at home in the body or away from it. For we must all appear before the judgment seat of Christ, so that each of us may receive what is due us for the things done while in the body, whether good or bad" (9-10). Paul teaches, what man does on earth will determine the reward he receives in Heaven. Then Paul writes, "Since, then, we know what it is to fear the Lord, we try to persuade others" (11). Paul also teaches, the fear of God should lead Christians to "persuade others." The fear of the Lord—the coming Judgment Seat of Christ is a motivation for sharing the gospel. Divine accountability, when understood and considered, is a biblical motivation for this project. This project will show that accountability in general is a great motivation for sharing the gospel on a regular basis.

The Case of Jesus

The case of Jesus is another biblical motivation for this project. Matthew writes, "Then he said to his disciples, 'The harvest is plentiful but the workers are few. Ask the Lord of the harvest, therefore, to send out workers into his harvest field'" (Mt. 9:37-38). The case of Jesus is clear. There are many people who need the Lord and there are only a few faithful disciples who are consistently engaged in sharing the gospel. This must change. Gene Edwards writes, "We dare not ever hope to win the world to Christ until we have regained a strong emphasis on personal witnessing."[95] The case of Jesus is a biblical motivation for regaining a strong emphasis on personal evangelism and for the need for this project.

The Experts Speak

There is no shortage of literature that supports the need for this project. There are books, articles, dissertations, and other great forms of literature that address the lack of zeal for personal evangelism in the church today and the lack of participation in personal evangelism by the same. The next few paragraphs will include a review of the top pieces of literature that influenced the author of this project to write on the researched problem. The bibliography includes a more exhaustive list of sources used; but the next few paragraphs will reveal the sources that had the greatest impact and influence on the author.

John Dickerson's book, *The Great Evangelical Recession,* is a must read for all current and soon to be ministry leaders and a book that highly reinforces the need for this project. It, like the evening news, contains a forecast church leaders need not miss. Senior pastor and bestselling author, Larry Osborne, adds, "I encourage every Christian leader to read the facts and the strategies John presents in *The Great Evangelical Recession.* This book will help prepare you for the future."[96] As the future approaches at warp speed, church leaders need to understand that preparation is necessary. Dickerson warns, "The American

---

95   Gene Edwards, *How to Have a Soul Winning Church.* (Springfield, Missouri: Gospel Publishing House): 56.

96   John S. Dickerson, *The Great Evangelical Recession.* (Grand Rapids, MI: Baker Publishing Group, 2013): back cover.

church is on the precipice of a spiritual recession."[97] Yes, there is a storm on the horizon and the church must get ready.

Dickerson presents six challenges facing the American church in the 21st Century. These challenges cannot be ignored. The challenges paint an accurate and disturbing picture of the current state of the American church. Dickerson also recommends six strategies for the church that desires to navigate the difficult times ahead in a way that will allow her to maximize her redemptive potential. The challenges Dickerson offers make the book worth reading. The strategies to address the challenges are a little weak, however they do provide a good overview of how a church can attack each challenge presented in the book. As a senior pastor and an award-winning journalist, Dickerson writes with much education and experience on the topic at hand. John McCandlish Phillips, a veteran *New York Times* journalist and author, adds, "John Dickerson is that rarity among evangelicals—a journalist of the highest capacity, but more than that, an analyst of breadth, insight, and laser-sharp foresight."[98] Dickerson's voice on the condition of the American church and the coming spiritual recession is a voice that should be heard. The book had such a profound impact on the author of this work he made it required reading for the pastoral staff his home church.

Lost in America How You and Your Church Can Impact the World Next Door by Tom Clegg and Warren Bird is another must read that heavily influenced the author in choosing the topic for this project and supports the need for the same. Clegg and Bird

---

97   Ibid, back cover.
98   Ibid, 1.

agree with John Dickerson, the aforementioned author, "Too many churches are becoming hopelessly irrelevant to the lost."[99] The message in the book is clear the American church must wake up and make some changes. Clegg and Bird also point out that "The Western world is the only major segment of the world's population in which Christianity is not growing."[100] The American church is losing ground in the mission of God. The church in America is no longer the beacon of light it once was in the world. Clegg and Bird are not simply prophets of doom. The authors offer some practical advice on how to be the change in this post-Christian America. The strategies in the book are relationally centered. Clegg and Bird write, "Relationships are absolutely central to God's purposes."[101] Each of the suggested strategies is designed to move the American church to make relationships with the lost a priority. Their message also points out the need for God's presence and power in the redemptive work of the American church. Franklin Graham adds, "*Lost in America* will help you identify fresh ways to relate the timeless message of Christ to searching people in your life today."[102] The author of this project agrees with Graham and made this book required reading for the ministry team at his home church.

One of the author's all-time favorite books on the biblical mandate for personal evangelism and the need for the same in the local church today is *How to Have A Soul Winning Church* by Gene Edwards. Gene Edwards has been one of the greatest

---

99   Tom Clegg and Warren Bird, *Lost in America: How You and Your Church Can Impact the World Next Door*, 3.

100   Ibid., 25.

101   Ibid., 56.

102   Ibid., back jacket cover.

influences on this author's life and on his decision making process for choosing this doctoral ministry project. *How to Have A Soul Winning Church* is a masterpiece and should be required reading for everyone who claims to know Christ as his personal Lord and Savior. The message of the book is clear and concise, "If ever we are to stop this undermining ourselves, our Lord, the Gospel, and even curtailing the effectiveness of the church building by our over emphasis of it, THEN WE MUST STOP INVITING THE LOST TO CHURCH, WE MUST START INVITING THEM TO CHRIST"[103] (original author's emphasis)!! The American church and all who make it up must personally engage in soul winning. Those who claim the name of Christ must share the gospel with those who are far from God.

The plan included in the book, *How to Have A Soul Winning Church,* to lead the church to personal evangelism may seem a little outdated for some. However, the intentionality and the urgency concerning a plan for personal evangelism must be caught and applied by the church or her influence in this post-Christian America will continue to wane and possibly cease to exist. While the book is strong on the need for intentionally engaging in the practice of personal evangelism, Edwards does not spend much time writing about the importance of building lasting relationships with lost people. Nevertheless, this book has greatly influenced the author in life and in the design of this work.

Hold the Rope Having a Heart for the Lost by Jeff Neal and Shonn Keels supports the need for this project. David Uth

---

103   Gene Edwards, 27.

writes, "In our effort to relate to the world, we have forgotten God has actually called us to go out and reach the lost. In a very straight forward and interesting way, *Hold the Rope*, gives us practical and Biblically grounded ways to get others close to Jesus."[104] Neal and Keels make it clear that following Jesus involves sharing Him with others who are far from God. After building the need for personal evangelism, Neal and Keels demonstrate a variety of ways the gospel can be shared with the lost. These men place a high priority on building relationships with lost people early in the book and continue emphasizing this principle throughout the book. They write, "Relationships are key and fundamental in sharing the Gospel."[105] The gospel itself emphasizes this truth. The gospel is all about relationship. God makes relationship with man possible through Christ. The church must never forget this important truth. Neal and Keels write, "Afterall, the Gospel flows best through the webs of relationships."[106] The church must leave the comforts of the sanctuary and make building relationships with the lost a priority. Then and only then will the church have a voice with those who are far from God. The need for a revival of personal evangelism is too great to be ignored. Countless numbers of lost people are counting on the church to get this right. *Hold the Rope* can help. This book emphasizes the need for personal evangelism and shares practical ways to engage in the same. This book may not be the complete answer for personal evangelism in the local

---

104 Jeff J. Neal and Shonn Keels, ix.
105 Ibid., 9.
106 Idib., 9.

church; but it can provide help for any church desiring to encourage and engage her people in the same. David Smith agrees, "If you're looking for a book that will motivate and inspire you toward personal evangelism … this is it!"[107] This author concurs with this assessment.

Leonard Ravenhill's *Why Revival Tarries* supports the need for a return to personal evangelism within the American church and the need for this project. Ravenhill writes, "An unprecedented tidal wave of commandment-breaking, God-defying, soul-destroying iniquity sweeps the ocean of human affairs. Never before have men in the masses sold their souls to the devil at such bargain prices."[108] America is spiritually bankrupt and the American church in many ways looks no different from those in popular culture. Ravenhill cries for revival and he asserts that revival is not possible apart from prayer. Much of his book is a call for the church to pray. Ravenhill writes, "The biggest single factor contributing to delayed Holy Ghost revival is this omission of soul travail. Revival tarries because we lack urgency in prayer."[109] Ravenhill's call to prayer is both biblical and necessary. As stated throughout this project, prayer is the fuel for faithful lives and fruitful personal evangelism. Even though Ravenhill does not directly call the church to return to the ministry of personal evangelism, he does acknowledge the need for it. Ravenhill writes, "The world is not looking for a new definition of the Gospel, but for a new demonstration of

---

107 Ibid., back cover.
108 Leonard Ravenhill, *Why Revival Tarries*. (Minneapolis, Minnesota: Bethany House, 1987): 93.
109 Ibid., 61.

the power of the Gospel."[110] This demonstration of the power of the gospel is Jesus alive in a believer's life. It is also Jesus proclaimed with the believer's lips. However, this demonstration is not possible apart from a dynamic prayer life.

Charles Spurgeon's timeless classic, *The Soul Winner*, supports the need for this project and has been a great motivation in the life of the author of this work. The book is a collection of lectures designed for seminary and Bible college students. Some of the greatest work on personal evangelism from the man affectionately known around the world as the "Prince of Preachers" is contained in this book. The overall message of the book can be summed up with the following excerpt:

> The objective of Christianity is not to educate men for their secular callings, or even to train them in the more refined arts and elegant professions, or to enable them to enjoy the beauties of nature or the charms of poetry. Jesus Christ did not come into the world for any of these things. He came "to seek and to save that which was lost" (Luke 19:10). He has sent His church on the same errand. She is a traitor to the Master who sent her if she is so beguiled by the beauties of taste and art as to forget that to "preach Christ, and Him crucified" (see 1 Corinthians 1:23, 2:2) is the only object for which she exists among the sons of men. The business of the church is the salvation of souls.[111]

---

110 Ibid., 46.
111 C.H. Spurgeon, *The Soul Winner*, (Louisville, Kentucky: GLH Publishing, 2015): 240-241.

The message could not be clearer. The church must engage in the activity of personal evangelism. The church must equip her people in personal evangelism and exhort her people in the practice of the same. Anything less is disobedience!

How to Win Souls & Influence People for Heaven by George Godfrey is another great source on personal evangelism that supports the need for this project. Godfrey writes, "Most Christians are not witnessing for the Lord Jesus Christ."[112] This statement alone supports the need for this project and summarizes the content of Godfrey's book. After Godfrey builds a biblical case for the need for Christians to engage in personal evangelism, he spends the rest of the book delivering an intentional plan for those who follow Christ to share the gospel on a regular basis. His plan includes a step-by-step process on how to lead someone to Christ and how to follow up with the new convert. Godfrey includes how to deal with difficulties and how to overcome fears. This is a great book. However, this book may be a tough read for the average church member. Nevertheless, the book is a great resource for this project.

True Evangelism also known as *Winning Souls by Prayer* in the revised edition by Lewis Sperry Chafer is a small but powerful book that supports the need for this project. *True Evangelism* especially influenced the author of this project concerning the chief obstacles to effective personal evangelism—the devil and the lack of prayer in evangelism. Chafer writes, "Because of the universal Satanic blindness upon the minds of unregenerate people (2 Cor. iv. 3, 4) the scope of the transforming work of

---

112 George Godfrey, *How to Win Souls and Influence People for Heaven.*
(Grand Rapids, Michigan: Baker Book House, 1973): 16.

salvation is not always understood, …"[113] Christians must never underestimate the work of the devil in the world today. The knowledge of such opposition must lead Christians everywhere to pray for God to demolish satanic strongholds so the gospel message can penetrate the hearts of the lost. Chafer adds, "Prayer presents the greatest opportunity for soul-winning, and there is precious reward promised to those who bring souls to Christ, and are found to be suffering with Him in His burden for the lost."[114] The devil is a real enemy to effective personal evangelism, and prayer is the greatest weapon in this war for souls. This book supports the great need for this project and reinforces the premises that the American church is failing in both personal evangelism and intentional prayer for the lost.

Jerry Wiles' book, *How to Win Others to Christ*, is another book that supports the need for this project. Wiles writes, "According to surveys, more than ninety percent of all Christians never lead even one person to Jesus Christ."[115] This statement is a resounding sad fact among all of the literature researched for this project. Christians are simply not sharing their faith in the Lord Jesus with people who are far from God. Personal evangelism has become a lost art in the American church. In the book, Wiles also points out the role of Christians in evangelism. The author makes it very clear that soul winners are simply vessels of God in which the gospel flows. Wiles writes, "You and I are God's instruments, used by Him to write living letters

---

113 Lewis Sperry Chafer, *True Evangelism or Winning Souls by Prayer*. (Findlay, Ohio: Dunham Publishing, 1919): 27.

114 Ibid., 93.

115 Jerry Wiles, *How to Win Others to Christ Your Personal, Practical Guide to Evangelism*. (Nashville, Tennessee: Thomas Nelson, 1992): 48.

of His love to this world."[116] This idea is in harmony with the apostle Paul's writings (1 Cor. 3:6). God is fully in control. The Christian is to be obedient and leave the results up to God.

Thom Rainer's book, *Surprising Insights from The Unchurched and Proven Ways to Reach Them,* supports the need for this ministry project. The book was written for the sole purpose of equipping ministry minded people and churches in how to reach the unchurched. C. Peter Wagner writes, "Here is a book like none other on how you can make the kind of adjustments in your church in order to maximize the harvest of the unchurched in your community."[117] It is clear that Rainer wrote this book to help churches and Christians maximize their Kingdom impact concerning reaching the unchurched. In *Surprising Insights*, Rainer shares several times that personal evangelism is not a dead method for reaching the unchurched. Rainer writes, "Joe entered the ranks of the formerly unchurched and became a Christian when three men personally evangelized him."[118] Personal evangelism works when Christians work it. However, Rainer adds, "Only one person is reached for Christ for every 85 church members in America."[119] This has to change! The church must wake up and answer the call of Christ to engage in personally reaching the lost. Rainer agrees,

> The formerly unchurched in our study left little doubt
> as to the importance of personal evangelism in reaching

---

116 Ibid., 5.
117 Thom Rainer, *Surprising Insights from the Unchurched and Proven Ways to Reach Them.* (Grand Rapids, Michigan: Zondervan, 2001): 3.
118 Ibid., 28.
119 Ibid., 36.

the unchurched. Over one-half indicated that someone from the church they joined shared Christ with them. Another 12 percent told us that someone other than a member at the church they joined personally evangelized them.[120]

The church cannot ignore this research or the Great Commission. This project is vital!

This project is necessary for TFC, churches all over America, and around the world. Personal evangelism must become a priority!

Growing True Disciples by George Barna supports the need for this project. Barna writes,

Here's a morsel of perspective. In one recent nationwide survey we asked people to describe their goals in life. Almost nine out of ten adults described themselves as "Christian." Four out of ten said they were personally committed to Jesus Christ, have confessed their sins and believed they were going to Heaven after they died because of God's grace provided through Jesus' death and resurrection. **And not one of the adults we interviewed said that their goal in life was to be a committed follower of Jesus Christ or to make disciples of the entire world—or even of their entire block**[121] (original author's emphasis).

---

120 Ibid., 43-44.

121 George Barna, *Growing True Disciples*, (Ventura, California: Issachar Resources, 2000): 11.

People who are truly committed to Jesus must be committed to His work. The lack of commitment by those who claim Christ compel the author of this project to prayerfully implement a plan to correct the problem and make disciples who make disciples who make disciples. Barna agrees, "Personal growth without reproduction is indefensible."[122] The mantra of the church is multiplication not addition.

Alphonse Turner did his doctoral work entitled, "A Personal Evangelism Training Plan" at Temple Baptist Seminary in North Carolina. Turner's doctoral ministry project supports the need for this work. Turner writes, "Many church leaders have struggled to motivate or revitalize evangelism in their churches."[123] The research for this project concurs with Turner's assessment. Too many churches are filled with members who are not actively engaged in personal evangelism and many pastors are not doing a great job reviving their churches in this area. Turner also writes, "Evangelism is one of the most important issues facing the church today."[124] There is no doubt in the truth of this statement. The population is increasing, and the church is losing ground. A revival in personal evangelism is necessary. Turner's project also addresses how many in the church are oblivious to this need. There is statistical data from Turner's immediate ministry context to support his claims. Overall, Turner presents a great plan to train his church members in personal evangelism and to motivate his members to do the same. The greatest impact Turner's work had on this author was

---

122 Ibid., 89.
123 Alphonse Turner Jr., "A Personal Evangelism Training Plan" (Doctoral diss. Temple Baptist Seminary, Fayetteville, North Carolina, 2013): vi.
124 Ibid., 1.

the research surrounding the need for personal evangelism in the American church today.

Thomas Roatch's doctoral dissertation entitled "Effective Personal Evangelism for Today's Church" supports the need for this project. Roatch agrees, "The importance of reaching and winning people to the Lord is an area that all Christians should be engaged and involved in."[125] The commission of the Lord Jesus to reach the lost is for all who call upon the name of the Lord. Christians who are not actively engaged in personal evangelism are living in disobedience. Roatch also does a great job communicating the role Christians play in evangelism and the role God plays in the same. Roatch writes, "Ultimately, only the Lord can change the situation or change a person's heart but He many times uses us to do this work."[126] This is a resounding truth. Christians need to obey—faithfully share the gospel with lost people; but God is ultimately in control of changing the hearts of the lost. Roatch's dissertation includes event evangelism and mass evangelism. While this is not wrong the author of this project will not address these forms of evangelism. Nevertheless, Roatch's work was a great read and a great encouragement to this author.

The Plan at The First Church

The plan to address the challenge at TFC is to add an effective ministry designed to equip people in personal evangelism and to incorporate an effective and culturally

---

125 Thomas M. Roatch, "Effective Personal Evangelism for Today's Church" Doctoral diss. (Liberty Baptist Theological Seminary, 2011): 3.
126 Ibid., 47.

relevant discipleship ministry. The plan will include a personal evangelism workshop that will be taught at the church in seminar style over the course of a weekend (See Appendix E). The plan will also include university style classes that cover the foundational teachings of the Christian faith. These classes are taught online by Luther Rice College and Seminary professors and can be taken at any time. These classes promote godly living and active engagement in personal evangelism. The workshop is designed to encourage and exhort members to participate faithfully in personal evangelism and equip members with a tool to help them share their faith. Over the past four years the young adult discipleship attendance and participation in personal evangelism at TFC have waned. As earlier mentioned, the conviction of the author is the two are related. Therefore, to change the attitudes and actions of the young adults concerning soul winning and to increase the personal evangelism efforts of the same, discipleship must be a priority!

The ongoing plan for TFC is to offer the personal evangelism workshop a couple of times a year. TFC will also encourage her membership to engage in the university style classes from Luther Rice online throughout the year as one's individual schedule permits. These classes are located on the following website: www.projectfocus.education. The classes and an explanation of the same are included in the appendices (See Appendix F). These online classes can be taken anytime. TFC has worked hard to remove any excuse that may keep people from engaging.

The plan as stated thus far is the ongoing plan for TFC to address the previously stated challenge within the young adult ministry concerning personal evangelism. However, the plan for this Doctor of Ministry project was conducted in a more controlled environment to ensure the required number of people necessary for the project actually completed the project. The timeline must be controlled to ensure the quantitative and qualitative research methods yield accurate results. The timeline for the project took place over the course of one month. The dates of the project are listed below. A detailed outline for the project is as follows.

I. The Teaching of Part One
of the Project for the Focus Group

Friday, January 3	5:00pm	Dinner at the Project Director's Home
	6:00pm	Pretest and Prequestionnaire
	6:30pm	4 Sessions God is Waiting to Meet You
	7:45pm	4 Sessions Engaging Your Finances
	9:00pm	4 Sessions Engaging Your World
	10:30pm	Hang out time
	12:00am	Lights out

II. The Teaching of Part Two
of the Project for the Focus Group

Saturday, January 4	8:00am	Breakfast at the Project Director's Home
	9:15am	4 Sessions Engaging the Word
	10:30am	4 Sessions God's Global Design

	11:45am	4 Sessions Ready to Engage
	1:00pm	Lunch at the Project Director's Home
	3:00pm	Session One
	4:00pm	Session Two
	5:00pm	Session Three
	6:00pm	Session Four
	7:00pm	Dinner at the Project Director's Home
	8:00pm	Sessions Five
	9:00pm	Session Six
	10:00pm	Dismiss back to your own home

III. One-Month Follow-Up for the Focus Group

Sunday, January 26	12:00pm	Lunch at the Project Director's House

(The Posttest and Postquestionnaire will be given.)

Mon-Fri, Jan 27—31	Post Interviews will be conducted.

The control group was given the same pretest and prequestionnaire on the Sunday the project was implemented with the focus group. The control group was also given the posttest and postquestionnaire on the Sunday of the one-month follow-up of the focus group. The focus group was given an exit interview. The control group was not given an exit interview. The results were measured, recorded, and added to this project.

CHAPTER THREE

THE IMPLEMENTATION
OF THE PLAN

Many thoughts and prayers have been employed concerning the implementation of the plan for this project. Many thoughts and prayers have also been employed concerning the methodology to be used in the implementation of this ministry project. Tim Sensing writes, "The term *methodology* is the overarching paradigm the research utilizes to study a particular problem"[127] (original author's emphasis). The importance of the methodology used in a project such as this one cannot be overstated. The methodology is vital in this project because the challenge at The First Church (TFC) is not an isolated challenge; rather the challenge is ubiquitous in the American church. Therefore, the methodology used in the implementation of the plan for this project will include both quantitative and qualitative research methods. The conviction of the author is that the use of these two methods will be complementary and

---

127 Tim Sensing, *Qualitative Research*. (Eugene, Oregon: Wipf & Stock, 2001): 26.

yield more comprehensive results. Explorable.com records, "If your study aims to find out, for example, what the dominant human behavior is towards a particular object or event and at the same time aims to examine why this is the case, it is then ideal to make use of both methods."[128] The employment of the quantitative and qualitative research methods will allow the project director to measure any changes in both the attitudes and the actions of the young adults at TFC in the area of personal evangelism. The use of both research methods will yield results that will help the project director answer the questions: what and why. The answers to these two questions are necessary to help the project director discern exactly how to address the challenge at TFC. The answers to these questions can also be used to help other churches throughout the United States and the world who are suffering from the same problem. Alphonse Turner states, "Many church leaders have struggled to motivate or revitalize evangelism in their churches."[129] The challenge at TFC is common among evangelical churches. As earlier stated, the challenge is, the majority of the membership of TFC is not actively engaged in sharing the gospel of the Lord Jesus Christ. Personal evangelism is no longer the priority. The membership has become comfortable with doing church rather than being the church. This challenge is an epidemic in the American church. The purpose of this project is to examine the young adults at TFC with particular reference to their lack of attention

---

128 "Quantitative and Qualitative Research. https://explorable.com/quantitative-and-qualitative-research, 2.

129 Alphonse Turner Jr., "A Personal Evangelism Training Plan" (Doctoral diss. Temple Baptist Seminary, Fayetteville, North Carolina, 2013): 12.

to and engagement in personal evangelism in order to develop a church-wide personal evangelism-training ministry. For this to happen, the project director must know what the attitudes of the young adults are concerning personal evangelism and why there is very little activity in the area of the same. The results of the quantitative and qualitative research methods that will be used in this project should yield the necessary data to provide the answers to these two questions. These answers will serve TFC, any church in America, and those around the world who choose to learn from them. These answers can help TFC and any church in America address the root challenges concerning the lack of attention to and involvement in personal evangelism. The answers will provide TFC and other churches insight that will be beneficial in building an effective church-wide evangelism-training ministry.

Data: The Project Director's Best Friend

Data is critical to the success of a ministry project. Tim Sensing agrees, "To be able to say anything in your thesis or to conclude something from your project, you need data."[130] Therefore the selection of tools to measure data is a critical step for any researcher. Certain tools deliver certain types of data. Sensing adds, "Once the research problem is determined and the intervention is implemented, you will need to decide what data will be required to evaluate the effectiveness of your action."[131] Understanding the importance of the selection of

---

130 Tim Sensing, *Qualitative Research*, 79.

131 Ibid., 79

the tools for a ministry project, much prayer and consideration were given to the selection of the tools that were employed in this ministry project. The tools selected are described in the next few paragraphs.

Tools for Gathering the Data

The quantitative method employed in this project made use of the following tools to gather measurable data to help discern the actions and attitudes of the young adults at TFC concerning personal evangelism: a pretest/posttest and prequestionnaire/postquestionnaire. The pretest/posttest and the prequestionnaire/postquestionnaire were given to both the focus group and the control group. The pretest/posttest is in Likert-scale form and consists of eleven statements. The prequestionnaire/postquestionnaire is a list of eight short-answer questions. According to Martyn Shuttleworth, using both a focus group and a control group allows for comparisons to be made in the research and in the results, "… giving them an idea of the overall effectiveness of the intervention or treatment."[132] These two tools yielded pertinent numerical data concerning the attitudes and actions of both the focus group and the control group that are recorded in graphs and charts. Shuttleworth adds, "Statistical analysis can then determine if the intervention had a significant effect."[133] The graphs and charts of the data are included in chapter four of this work.

---

132 Martyn Shuttleworth, "Pretest-Posttest Designs." Explorable,
      November 3, 2009. https://explorable.com/pretest-posttest-designs.
133 Ibid.

The qualitative research method used in this project made use of an exit interview of each participant in the focus group from the young adult ministry at TFC as the primary tool for gathering pertinent information. The control group was not given an exit interview. Each exit interview has been recorded. The exit interview is necessary. Sensing agrees, "The main purpose of the interview is to obtain a special kind of information."[134] The project director used the exit interview to measure this special kind of information that cannot be gathered through any other method—matters of the heart. Heart matters, an individual's thoughts, values, and feelings are more likely to be discovered in an interview than any other research instrument. David Guthrie agrees, "Qualitative research provides a way of drawing or teasing out the truths that govern individual behaviors in particular situations."[135] Interviews give more information than what can be obtained through observation alone. The extra insight gained through interviews can be vital to the overall project especially in measuring the attitudes behind one's actions. Sensing agrees, "A researcher might arrive at certain conclusions through observation that will be confirmed, modified, or even corrected through interviews."[136] The interviews can help remove certain biases that may be held by the project director and help produce more accurate results. The results of the exit interviews have been recorded.

134   Tim Sensing, *Qualitative Research*. 104.
135   David Alexander Guthrie, "Issues Effecting Church Membership: A Case Study Examining the Vocation of Sharing the Gospel" Doctoral diss. (St. Stephen's College, Edmonton, Alberta,): 28.
136   Tim Sensing, *Qualitative Research*. 103.

The Plan for the Intervention

After receiving approval for the aforementioned project, ten young adults from TFC were invited to be a part of the focus group. Another ten young adults were invited to be a part of the control group. The ten young adults in the focus group took the pretest and filled out the prequestionnaire according to the schedule listed in chapter two of this work. Upon completing both of these quantitative measuring tools, each of the young adults in the focus group participated in the intervention that was held in the home of the project director in the format of an intensive discipleship weekend. The resources that were used in this project are: an evangelism workshop created by the project director (See Appendix E) and six online classes from Luther Rice College (See Appendix F). The resources used in such a project were vital to the outcome of the same. Much prayer and consideration were given concerning the selection of these resources because of how important resources are to the success of a project. Sensing agrees, "A lack of resources will hamper if not doom your project."[137] Again, the selection of these resources is the result of much prayer, consideration, and research. During the intensive discipleship weekend, the focus group completed all six online courses from Luther Rice and the personal evangelism workshop. The ten young adults in the control group were given the exact same pretest and prequestionnaire during their Sunday school hour; but they did not take the online courses from Luther Rice nor did they attend the personal evangelism workshop. The ten young adults in the focus group completed the posttest and the postquestionnaire

---

137   Ibid., 27.

one month after the completion of the six online Luther Rice courses and the personal evangelism workshop (See schedule in chapter two). The ten young adults in the control group completed the same posttest and the same postquestionnaire at the same time as the focus group during their Sunday school hour. The ten young adults in the focus group were administered an exit interview five weeks after completing the six online Luther Rice courses and the personal evangelism workshop (See schedule in chapter two).

The Hypothesis

The hypothesis is that the young adults in the focus group will experience a greater and more positive change in their attitudes and actions concerning personal evangelism. The project director also believes that a good percentage of the focus group will engage in personal evangelism before the project ends. The hypothesis concerning the control group is there will likely be little change in the attitudes and actions of those in the control group. The results of the collected data were recorded, measured, and studied. Sensing warns, "Data collection is a critical issue for the project. If not done well, the whole process will be jeopardized."[138] Understanding the importance of Sensing's warning, the project director employed the help of his administrative assistant to collect and record all of the data. A copy of the test (pretest/posttest) is included (See Appendix G). A copy of the questionnaire (prequestionnaire/ postquestionnaire) is also included (See Appendix H). A copy of the interview that was given five weeks after completion of the

---

138 Ibid., 90.

online courses from Luther Rice and the personal evangelism workshop is also included (See Appendix I).

The project took place in the home of the project director, and it required a budget. Sensing writes, "Many DMin projects will not require funds outside the normal operating budgets of the church or organization."[139] Such is the case in this project. The budget for the project was four hundred dollars, and it was absorbed in TFC's discipleship budget. The focus group was fed supper on the opening night. The focus group was also fed, breakfast, lunch, supper, and snacks on day two of the project. On the Sunday of week five following the intervention the focus group was fed lunch at the project director's home. The meals included: chicken bog for supper and snacks on the first night. On day two, the focus group was provided: cereal for breakfast, sandwiches and chips for lunch, and grilled hamburgers for supper. Five weeks after the intervention, the focus group was provided spaghetti for lunch. The wife of the project director graciously assisted the project director in cooking all of the meals for the focus group.

The project director and the young adult pastor at TFC worked together on the selection of the focus group. The selection of the focus group largely depended on the availability of the ten young adults selected. The control group consisted of ten young adults from the young adult class that were not selected to be a part of the focus group. All members of the focus group and the control group are active members of the young adult ministry at TFC. The employment of a control group for this project was vital to the success of the project.

---

139 Ibid., 27.

Martyn Shuttleworth and Lyndsay Wilson agree, "A scientific control group is an essential part of many research designs, allowing researchers to minimize the effect of variables except the independent variable. The control group, receiving no intervention, is used as a baseline to compare groups and assess the effect of that intervention."[140] The control group helped demonstrate that any changes measured in the actions and attitudes in the focus group above and beyond that of the control group were indeed a result of the project. The use of the control group provided the opportunity for significant comparisons to be charted.

Ethical Considerations

Ethics is vital to the health of this project. Soyini Madison writes, "Ethics is concerned with the principles of right and wrong. Questions of morality and what it means to be honorable, to embrace goodness, to perform virtuous acts, to generate goodwill, and to choose justice above injustice constitute the study of ethics."[141] Because of these important factors, certain steps were taken to ensure proper ethical standards were maintained throughout the project. The first step the project director took to ensure trust with the participants was built from the beginning as he shared in the orientation only first names were used throughout the project. The second step is the project director made clear the information obtained throughout the

140   Martyn Shuttleworth and Lyndsay T. Wilson, (Jun 16, 2010). Scientific Control Group. Retrieved Oct 18, 2019 from Explorable. com: https://explorable.com/scientific-control-group.
141   Soyini D. Madison, *Critical Ethnography*. (Thousand Oaks, California: Sage, 2005): 80.

project will be made available for the public to read and study. The third step the project director took was he made sure the participants understood all of the information obtained throughout the project would also be stored on his password protected computer. The final and most important step that was taken is the use of informed consent. Sensing writes, "Informed consent involves a set of practices designed to give everyone connected to the project the information they need to decide whether to participate in the project."[142] Openness and honesty are key ethical markers that were demonstrated throughout the project. The informed consent helped lay this foundation for all who agreed to be involved. Bruce Berg agrees, "*Informed consent* means the knowing consent of individuals to participate as an exercise of their choice, free from any element of fraud, deceit, duress, or similar unfair inducement or manipulation"[143] (original author's emphasis). The project director ensured there were no secrets or hidden agendas. While the relationship of the project director with each participant is one of a pastor and a Christian, the project director did not take his role of shepherd for granted. Instead, the project director took steps to ensure the highest ethical standards were met for this project, such as the use of informed consent. The informed consent included a statement informing each participant of his right to remove himself at any time if he became uncomfortable during the project. The informed consent was read and signed by each participant and returned to the project director before

---

142 Tim Sensing, *Qualitative Research*. 34.
143 Bruce L. Berg, *Qualitative Research Methods for the Social* Sciences. 3rd ed. (Boston, Massachusetts: Allyn and Bacon, 1988): 47.

the project started. A copy of the informed consent is included in the appendices (See Appendix K). A cover letter with an invitation to participate in the focus group for the ministry project was attached to the front of the informed consent (See Appendix J). A copy of the previously stated schedule was also attached to the cover letter and informed consent for the focus group to look over before signing and returning the informed consent.

The Most Valuable People

The implementation of this project required the help of certain individuals. Sensing agrees, "You will not be conducting your research in a vacuum."[144] The project consisted of two separate groups of ten persons: a control group and a focus group. The young adult pastor assisted the project director in selecting the participants for these two groups. The project director and his wife hosted the ten members of the focus group in their home according to the previously stated schedule of the project. The wife of the project director also helped cook for the focus group according to the same schedule. The project director's administrative assistant helped collect and record all data. The administrative assistant also helped the project director in transferring the results of the collected data into charts and graphs that were recorded, analyzed, and studied. TFC absorbed any and all monetary requirements for the project. There are others who are not mentioned here that prayed for the project to be: God honoring, Christ exalting, and Spirit-led. These faithful church members are also praying for the project

---

144 Tim Sensing, *Qualitative Research*. 27.

to bear much fruit that will have a lasting impact on TFC and the Kingdom of God for years to come. Finally, David Hancock and the team at Morgan James Publishing turned this project into a published book that will influence the global church for years to come.

Evaluation: The Breakfast of Champions

Evaluation is the breakfast of those who make a difference in life. Feedback is essential to success. Tim Sensing agrees, "Once the intervention has been implemented, you will need to assess the outcomes or changes to see how the intervention accomplished its task."[145] Simply put, an evaluation of the ministry project is necessary to the overall success of the same. Michael Quinn Patton defines evaluation as, "… the systematic collection, analysis, and interpretation of information about the activities, characteristics, and outcomes of actual programs in order to make judgments about specific aspects of the program, improve the program's effectiveness, and make decisions about the program's future."[146] Without this pertinent step of evaluation, the hours spent in research were in vain and the project would bear little to no fruit. The evaluation was necessary to determine the validity of the intervention and how the intervention can be used in the future to reach certain desired ministry goals. The evaluation of this ministry project was determined by the executive ministry team at TFC, which consisted of the senior pastor, the associate pastor (who

---

145 Ibid., 70.

146 Michael Quinn Patton, *How to Use Qualitative Methods in Evaluation.* (Thousand Oaks, California, 1987): 145.

is the project director), and the executive pastor. These men have provided three angles of vision for reading the data. Tim Sensing writes, "Any single approach will have limitations."[147] The senior pastor has provided the insider's angle of vision. The associate pastor has provided the researcher's angle of vision. The executive pastor has provided the outsider's angle of vision.

While the executive pastor is not involved in the day-to-day ministry of the church, he works directly with the finances and the facilities of the church and will faithfully fulfill the role of the outsider. These men have prayerfully studied the data recorded from the research project to help determine the future path for an ongoing effective church-wide evangelism-training ministry to ensure the membership of TFC is faithful to the "Great Commission" of the Lord Jesus. These men are determined that TFC will become a church committed to reaching and growing people in the name of the Lord Jesus Christ. These men desire that soul winning once again become a top priority in this church. These men agree it is time we intentionally lead God's people to *Go Fish*!

---

147 Tim Sensing, *Qualitative Research*. 72.

CHAPTER FOUR

THE RESULTS OF THE PROJECT

The project took place according to the previously stated schedule included at the end of chapter two. The data gathered and the information gained during this project indicate the intervention is a success, and they are presented in the rest of this chapter. First, there is the data from the pretest for the control group and then from the focus group. Listed next is a comparison of the results of the pretest between the two groups. It is clear from the pretest results that both the control group and the focus group are on fairly level ground with their attitudes and actions concerning personal evangelism. Included next is a side-by-side comparison of the control group and the focus group based on the prequestionnaire. There were three notable differences discovered between the two groups in the prequestionnaire. According to the answers given to question three on the prequestionnaire, the focus group is far more active in Bible study outside of Sunday school than the control group. According to the answers given to question seven on the prequestionnaire, the focus group is also far more active in Scripture memory when compared to the control group. However, at this point, these commitments to the study of Scripture and the memorization of the same do not appear to have any direct impact on the focus group's commitment to personal evangelism when compared to the personal evangelism habits of the control group. According to the answers given to question eight, the control group is far more faithful to the discipline of accountability in the area of personal evangelism than the focus group. However, at this point, the practice of accountability in the control group also does not appear to have any significant impact on the control group's commitment to personal evangelism. Included next is a side-by-side comparison of the prequestionnaire results of the control group and focus group followed by a comparison graph of these results.

The next part of this chapter contains the data gathered from the results of the focus group one month after the intervention took place. Listed first is a graph comparing the pretest/posttest results of the focus group. Listed next is a graph comparing the prequestionnaire/postquestionnaire results of the focus group. Finally, the information gained from the exit interviews of the focus group is listed. The information gained from these two measuring tools along with the information gained from the exit interviews contain some of the most important information of the entire project. This information will be used to determine the value of the intervention. Without this information, the value of the intervention would be impossible to ascertain.

The information gained from the posttest and postquestionnaire of the control group yields very little change. The changes are so insignificant, they are not included in this chapter. The pre-intervention data gathered from the control group was a great help when compared to the pre-intervention data of the focus group; however, the post-intervention data does not offer any significant help. Therefore, the project director will focus on the differences made in the focus group only when evaluating the success of the intervention. At this point, it should be noted, the insignificant changes measured in the control group are a strong indication the intervention yields positive results. This fact will be explained later in the chapter when the results of the focus group are revealed.

Control Group: Pretest Results

Statement Number One:

Christians regularly participate in personal evangelism.

The data reveals eighty percent of the control group has a good grasp concerning the truth that evangelism is indeed a challenge in the evangelical church in the United States. The project director is surprised by the result of this data considering the fact that the majority of the control group is not regularly involved in personal evangelism. The convictions of the group in this matter do not match their practice nor are their convictions consistent with research. Most of the research studied for this project indicates the average Christian is oblivious to the lack of participation in personal evangelism within the American evangelical church.

Statement Number Two:

Christians believe personal evangelism is their responsibility.

The data indicates one hundred percent of the control group believes Christians understand that personal evangelism is the responsibility of every believer in Christ. This conviction is contrary to the research discovered in this project and shared in the introduction of the same. The project director's claim that many in the church are oblivious to the lack of concern surrounding personal evangelism is supported by this erroneous conviction of the control group; or the church is aware, and the church does not care.

Statement Number Three:

I participated in personal evangelism within the last week.

According to the data sixty percent of the control group is not actively sharing their faith. It also appears the other forty percent is not sure if they really shared their faith. No one indicates with certainty that personal evangelism is a common practice. This data is consistent with the project director's hypothesis that only a small percentage of the evangelical church regularly participates in personal evangelism.

Statement Number Four:

Getting a conversion is the responsibility of the one doing the personal evangelism.

The data indicates eighty percent of the control group understands that changing a heart is the work of the Holy Spirit.

The data also reveals that twenty percent of the control group does not fully understand that simply sharing one's faith is considered successful evangelism—obedience, and the business of changing a heart is solely the responsibility of God. This information is somewhat encouraging. A correct understanding of the ministry of the Holy Spirit will give confidence in personal evangelism.

<u>Statement Number Five</u>:

Personal evangelism is appropriate in a work environment.

According to the data one hundred percent of the control group believes personal evangelism should be an accepted practice in the workplace. However, the results reveal, not many of them are practicing this privilege. There is an obvious disconnect between belief and practice in the control group concerning this statement.

<u>Statement Number Six</u>:

I am successful each time I participate in personal evangelism regardless of the listener's response.

The data reveals seventy percent of the control group understands that obedience in personal evangelism is success in the same. According to the aforementioned response to statement number three, at least seventy percent of the control group acknowledges they are living in disobedience concerning personal evangelism. The lack of engagement in personal evangelism is not surprising when compared to the research for this project. However, the acknowledgement that the lack of involvement is disobedience, and this acknowledgement has little impact on the same is disturbing.

Statement Number Seven:

I am involved in a regularly scheduled Bible study class outside of Sunday school.

According to the data at least seventy percent of the control group is not involved in a study of the Scripture outside of Sunday school. Only thirty percent of the control group appears to be involved in Bible study throughout the week. This claim is consistent with the project director's hypothesis that people who do not regularly study the Bible do not regularly engage in personal evangelism. The old adage appears to be true, growing people grow people.

Statement Number Eight:

I typically think about the lostness of people.

The data reveals ninety percent of the control group is somewhat bothered by the lostness around them, yet not many of them are doing anything about it. The project director is surprised by the results of this data. The apparent concern for the lost within the control group does not match the involvement in personal evangelism of the same. Thoughts typically lead to action.

Statement Number Nine:

I read my Bible daily.

The data indicates only sixty percent of the control group reads the Bible consistently. This is disturbing especially considering the control group is made up of members of the church that are considered to be very active members. More than fifty percent of the group actively serves on a ministry team within the church. This group represents those who make up the core of TFC; yet they are not reading the Scripture daily.

Statement Number Ten:

I have a lost friend that I pray for daily.

The data collected concerning this statement is very encouraging considering the importance of prayer in personal evangelism. According to the data sixty percent of the control group prays for a lost friend weekly. This is great. However, the results appear to be a little high in comparison to the inactivity within the control group concerning personal evangelism. Nevertheless, the results are what the pretest revealed. It seems that those who think about lost people and pray specifically for a lost person or lost people would be engaging in personal evangelism at some point. However, the data did not indicate this to be the norm.

Statement Number Eleven:

I have a lost friend that I meet with regularly.

Understanding the gospel flows best through the webs of relationships raises a great concern when considering the results of the data concerning this statement. The data indicates eighty percent of the control group is not growing in a friendship with a lost person. Based on research, this is typical of the evangelical church in the United States today.

Those who claim to know Christ tend to spend time with those who are like them. This data seems out of place after studying the data of the prior two statements. Members of the control group are concerned about the lost and praying for the lost; yet they are not growing in a friendship with someone who is lost. While this data seems contradictory, the information is correct according to the pretest.

Focus Group: Pretest Results

<u>Statement Number One</u>:

Christians regularly participate in personal evangelism.

According to the data seventy percent of the focus group has a good grasp on the truth that evangelism is indeed a challenge in the evangelical church in the United States. There is little variance between the control group and the focus group with their convictions concerning statement one. Both groups understand the majority of the church is silent when it comes to personally sharing the gospel with the lost.

<u>Statement Number Two</u>:

Christians believe personal evangelism is their responsibility.

The data indicates sixty percent of the focus group believes that Christians understand that personal evangelism is the responsibility of every believer in Christ. The conviction of the focus group is a little more consistent with reality when compared to the conviction of the control group. However, based on the research for this project, the focus group as a whole still possesses an erroneous conviction when compared to the current context of the evangelical church in the United States. Research indicates most Christians believe personal evangelism is for the supposed spiritually elite not for the average church member.

Statement Number Three:

I participated in personal evangelism within the last week.

The data reveals seventy percent of the focus group is not actively sharing their faith. It also appears that twenty percent is not sure if they really shared their faith. Only one person (10%) indicates that he definitely shares his faith. It should be noted that the young man who shares his faith attends a Baptist college and is good friends with some of the football players at his school who do not know Jesus. There is little variance between the control group and the focus group with their conviction concerning statement three. This is disappointing.

Statement Number Four:

Getting a conversion is the responsibility of the one doing the personal evangelism.

According to the data forty percent of the focus group understands that changing a heart is the work of the Holy Spirit. The data also indicates sixty percent of the control group does not fully understand that simply sharing one's faith is considered successful evangelism—obedience, and the business of changing hearts is the responsibility of God. The focus group has a better grasp on this truth when compared to the control group.

Statement Number Five:

Personal evangelism is appropriate in a work environment.

The data indicates eighty percent of the focus group believes that personal evangelism should be an accepted practice in the workplace. The conviction of the focus group is twenty percent less than that of the control group concerning this truth. However, the greater surprise is two very committed young adults believe the workplace is off limits for a believer to share his faith. This is disheartening!

Statement Number Six:

I am successful each time I participate in personal evangelism regardless of the listener's response.

The data reveals eighty percent of the focus group understands obedience in personal evangelism is success in the same. The conviction of the focus group is ten percent higher than that of the control group concerning this truth. However, this conviction does not appear to have any impact on the focus group's involvement in personal evangelism. A proper understanding of one's role in personal evangelism should lead people to action.

Statement Number Seven:

I am involved in a regularly scheduled Bible study class outside of Sunday school.

According to the data eighty percent of the focus group engages in a Bible study outside of Sunday school. Again, only thirty percent of the control group appears to be involved in

Bible study throughout the week. This is a noticeable difference. However, according to the data concerning statement number three, this difference does not indicate any substantial change in the practice of personal evangelism within the focus group. Both groups are fairly inactive in the area of personal evangelism.

<u>Statement Number Eight</u>:
I typically think about the lostness of people.

The data reveals one hundred percent of the focus group is bothered by the lostness of the people around them. At first glance, the results of this data are very encouraging. However, when considered in light of all of the data, these results are not as encouraging; because like the control group, not many of the focus group are doing anything about it on a consistent basis. As earlier stated, thoughts should lead to action. However, this is not the case according to the results of this statement. This information is also disappointing.

<u>Statement Number Nine</u>:
I read my Bible daily.

According to the data, ninety percent of the focus group studies the Bible daily or at least regularly. This is a fifty percent increase in practice over the control group and is consistent with the data concerning statement number seven. The data reveals the focus group is more involved in Bible study and the reading of the Bible. However, the personal evangelism practice of the focus group is similar to the control group. There is very little difference between the two groups in the area of sharing the gospel. This information is disturbing. The project director's hypothesis and the research for this project include the conviction that growing people are involved in personal evangelism. At this point in the project, the data does not support this hypothesis.

<u>Statement Number Ten</u>:

I have a lost friend that I pray for daily.

According to the data seventy percent of the focus group prays for a lost friend daily or at least regularly. There is little variance between the control group and the focus group with their conviction concerning statement ten. The practice of praying for the lost appears to have little impact on the personal evangelism habits of either group. This must change. Praying for the lost should move people toward personal evangelism. Again, it must be noted that this information is contrary to the information gained from the reading and research for this project. Most of the reading and research support the hypothesis that people who are committed to praying for lost people are more likely to be actively engaged in personal evangelism.

<u>Statement Number Eleven</u>:

I have a lost friend that I meet with regularly.

The data indicates seventy percent of the focus group is not growing in a friendship with a lost person. There is little variance between the control group and the focus group with their conviction concerning statement eleven. Again, like with the control group, this is very disappointing. Relationships are key in personal evangelism. Christians are not called to be of the world; but they are called to live in the world. Light must invade the darkness. Building relationships with lost people will be key for anyone wanting to make a difference through personal evangelism. The hope is the intervention will help the focus group understand how important building relationships with lost people is in the area of personal evangelism.

The following chart reflects a comparison between the control group and the focus group based on the above initial responses to the pretest that was given before the focus group received the intervention to address the defined challenge. The vertical axis reaches one hundred percent as a maximum (desired) score for each statement included on the pretest. The horizontal axis represents the eleven statements on the pretest in order.

Pretest Comparison Between the Control Group and the Focus Group

Statement	Control Group	Focus Group
One	80%	70%
Two	0%	40%
Three	40%	30%
Four	80%	40%
Five	90%	80%
Six	70%	80%
Seven	30%	80%
Eight	90%	100%
Nine	60%	90%
Ten	60%	70%
Eleven	20%	30%

Control Group and Focus Group Comparison from Prequestionnaire:

Question # 1:

When was the last time you shared the gospel with someone? (Briefly explain).

According to the data fifty percent of the control group has been active in personal evangelism within the last year at least once. The data also indicates sixty percent of the focus group has been active in personal evangelism within the last year at least once. There is very little variance between the two groups concerning the activity of the members from each group in personal evangelism. This information is consistent when compared with the data from the pretest on the activity of personal evangelism.

Question #2:

Who is primarily responsible for sharing the gospel? Why? (Briefly explain).

Both groups have a great understanding of who is responsible for sharing the gospel. The data indicates one hundred percent of the control group believes all Christians have been commanded by the Lord Jesus to share their faith regularly. This unanimous conviction is contrary to the research documented in the genesis of this project; however, it is encouraging. The data also reveals one hundred percent of the focus group also believes all Christians have been commanded by the Lord Jesus to engage in personal evangelism. There is no variance between the two groups concerning this question.

While this solid conviction from both groups is atypical when compared to national statistics, it is not surprising considering each group member is a member of The First Church (TFC). The responsibility and privilege for all Christians to engage in personal evangelism is regularly taught and preached at TFC. However, it is disturbing that this unanimous conviction is not leading many of the group members to consistently build relationships with the lost and share the gospel.

Question #3:

How often are you involved in studying the Bible weekly? (Briefly explain).

According to the data only fifty percent of the control group studies the Bible outside of Sunday school. The data also indicates one hundred percent of the focus group studies the Bible outside of Sunday school. There is a substantial difference in the commitment level to study God's word between the control group and the focus group. However, at this point, the difference in commitment levels does not appear to have a significant impact on personal evangelism. This information is contrary to earlier research done for this project.

Question #4:

What is the gospel? (Briefly explain).

Both groups have a great grasp on the definition of the gospel. The data indicates one hundred percent of the control group clearly understands how to succinctly explain the gospel to someone. The data also reveals one hundred percent of the focus group also understands how to succinctly explain the gospel to someone. This is both encouraging and disappointing. It is encouraging that many truly understand who Jesus is and what Jesus has done for them. It is also disappointing because only a few of these people are actually sharing the gospel on a consistent basis. Again, the knowledge of the gospel within both groups is not surprising considering the strong gospel teaching and preaching at TFC.

Question # 5:

What are some verses that can be used in sharing the gospel? Why? (Briefly explain).

According to the data ninety percent of the control group has memorized specific verses designed to help them to share the gospel with a lost person. The data also indicates ninety percent of the focus group has memorized specific verses designed to help them in personal evangelism. Again, this is both encouraging and disappointing. It is encouraging that each group is memorizing Scripture. However, it is discouraging that the practice of Scripture memorization does not appear to be impacting their practice of personal evangelism.

Question #6:

Who are you currently praying that God will bring to salvation? (Briefly explain the relationship to this person or these people).

Both groups appear to understand the need for believers to pray for the lost. The data reveals one hundred percent of the control group regularly prays for at least one lost friend or family member. The data also indicates one hundred percent of the focus group also regularly prays for at least one lost friend or family member. There is no variance concerning this question between the control group and the focus group. This information is surely encouraging. However, it must be noted, at this point, regularly praying for a lost person or lost people is having little impact on the personal evangelism habits of either group.

Question #7:

What are the last four verses you memorized and when? (Briefly explain).

According to the data only twenty percent of the control group regularly participates in Scripture memory. The data also reveals fifty percent of the focus group regularly participates in Scripture memory. The focus group is more committed in memorizing Scripture. However, at this point, the memorization of Scripture does not appear to have a direct impact on personal evangelism.

Question #8:

Who regularly holds you accountable to share the gospel? How? (Briefly explain).

The project director believes accountability is important in life and in personal evangelism. He did not find information on accountability in personal evangelism in his research for this project. However, the data collected before and after the intervention indicates accountability is important. According to the data, sixty percent of the control group claims to have an accountability partner in the area of personal evangelism. The data also reveals the focus group does not have any accountability in the area of personal evangelism. At this point in the research for the project, accountability appears to be a missing link.

The following chart reflects a comparison between the control group and the focus group based on the above initial responses to the prequestionnaire that was given before the focus group received the intervention to address the defined challenge. The vertical axis reaches one hundred percent as a maximum (desired) score for each question included in the prequestionnaire. The horizontal axis represents the eight questions in the prequestionnaire in order. Notable differences between the two groups are discovered in questions three, seven, and eight. The differences indicate the control group is stronger in the area of accountability while the focus group is more committed to the disciplines of Bible study and the memorization of Scripture. While the differences in the answers to these three questions are great, they do not appear to have a major influence in how often the gospel is being shared by either group. About fifty-five percent of both groups combined have shared the gospel in the last month and thirty-five percent of them have shared the gospel in the last week (This is high compared to the national average).

Prequestionnaire Comparison Between
the Control Group and the Focus Group

Question	Control-Pre	Focus-Pre
One	50%	60%
Two	100%	100%
Three	50%	100%
Four	100%	100%
Five	90%	90%
Six	100%	100%
Seven	20%	50%
Eight	0%	60%

The chart below reflects a comparison of the focus group's responses to the pretest and the posttest and contains some of the most important information in this project. The data reflects positive changes in eight of the eleven statements. There was no change in two of the statements and in one statement there is a minor negative change. The vertical axis reaches one hundred percent as a maximum (desired) score for each statement included on the pretest. The horizontal axis represents the eleven statements on the pretest/posttest in order. The eleven statements are again included below the chart for quick reference.

Pretest and Posttest Comparison of the Focus Group

Statement	Focus-Pretest	Focus-Posttest
One	70%	60%
Two	40%	60%
Three	30%	50%
Four	40%	50%
Five	80%	100%
Six	80%	100%
Seven	80%	80%
Eight	100%	100%
Nine	90%	100%
Ten	70%	100%
Eleven	30%	40%

Pretest Statements:

1. Christians regularly participate in personal evangelism.
2. Christians believe personal evangelism is their responsibility.
3. I participated in personal evangelism with the last week.
4. Getting a conversion is the responsibility of the one doing personal evangelism.
5. Personal evangelism is appropriate in a work environment.
6. I am successful each time I participate in personal evangelism regardless of the listener's response.
7. I am involved in a regularly scheduled Bible study class outside of Sunday school.
8. I typically think about the lostness of people.

9. I read my Bible daily.
10. I have a lost friend that I pray for daily.
11. I have a lost friend that I meet with regularly.

Prequestionnaire and Postquestionnaire comparison of the Focus Group:

Question # 1:

When was the last time you shared the gospel with someone? (Briefly explain).

The prequestionnaire data indicates sixty percent of the focus group has been active in personal evangelism within the last year at least once. The postquestionnaire data reveals seventy percent of the focus group has been active in personal evangelism in the past year. There has been a slight increase in activity since the intervention. This is a small step in the right direction.

Question #2:

Who is primarily responsible for sharing the gospel? Why? (Briefly explain).

According to the prequestionnaire data one hundred percent of the focus group believes all Christians have been commanded by the Lord Jesus to share their faith regularly. The postquestionnaire data also indicates one hundred percent of the focus group also believes all Christians have been commanded by the Lord Jesus to engage in personal evangelism. There is no variance in the data concerning this question.

Question #3:

How often are you involved in studying the Bible weekly? (Briefly explain).

The prequestionnaire data indicates one hundred percent of the focus group studies the Bible outside of Sunday school. The postquestionnaire data also reveals one hundred percent of the focus group studies the Bible outside of Sunday school. There is no variance in the data concerning this question. The data indicates the focus group is very committed to the reading and the studying of God's word. The intervention had no effect on this group in this area.

Question #4:

What is the gospel? (Briefly explain).

According to the prequestionnaire data one hundred percent of the focus group also understands how to succinctly explain the gospel to someone. The postquestionnaire data also indicates one hundred percent of the focus group understands how to succinctly explain the gospel to someone. There is no variance in the data concerning this question. This is very encouraging. The apostle Paul teaches there is power in the gospel and that without hearing it one cannot be saved (Rom. 1:16 & 10:17). The focus group has a great grasp on the content of the gospel message.

Question # 5:

What are some verses that can be used in sharing the gospel? Why? (Briefly explain).

The prequestionnaire data indicates ninety percent of the focus group has memorized specific verses designed to help them in personal evangelism. The postquestionnaire data reveals one hundred percent of the focus group has memorized specific verses designed to help them in personal evangelism. This is a slight positive increase since the intervention.

Question #6:

Who are you currently praying that God will bring to salvation? (Briefly explain your relationship to this person or these people).

According to the prequestionnaire data one hundred percent of the focus group regularly prays for at least one lost friend or family member. The post questionnaire data also indicates one hundred percent of the focus group regularly prays for at least one lost friend or family member. There was no variance in the data concerning this question. The focus group consistently prays for lost people. This is a necessary discipline.

Question #7:

What are the last four verses you memorized and when? (Briefly explain).

According to David, Scripture memory is important for daily living (Ps. 119:11). It is also helpful in personal evangelism. The prequestionnaire data reveals fifty percent of the focus group regularly participates in Scripture memory. The postquestionnaire data indicates sixty percent of the focus group participates in Scripture memory. This is a slight move in the right direction.

Question #8:

Who regularly you accountable to share the gospel? How? (Briefly explain).

The prequestionnaire data indicates the focus group does not have any accountability in the area of personal evangelism. The postquestionnaire data reveals forty percent of the focus group now has someone holding them accountable in the area of personal evangelism. **This is the most significant change according to the results of the data from the questionnaire.** This is a move in the right direction. **Again, accountability appears to be a missing link in the area of personal evangelism.**

The practice of accountability in personal evangelism was absent in the research done for this project. This was not by design. There simply was no information discovered from the extensive study done by the project director. However, the project director has also done a separate personal experiment in the area of accountability to discern its impact on personal evangelism. The staff he observed at TFC now includes accountability in the area of personal evangelism in their weekly staff meeting. This has not always been the case. However, since the genesis of this project the staff at TFC has recognized they are not very evangelistic personally. The accountability that has been added to the staff meeting has increased the staff's involvement in personal evangelism.

The following chart reflects a comparison of the above responses of the focus group to the prequestionnaire/postquestionnaire. The vertical axis reaches one hundred percent as a maximum (desired) score for each question included in the questionnaire. The horizontal axis represents the eight questions listed in the questionnaire in the order in which they were given. The differences that took place as a result of the intervention are visible. While there are a few slight changes in the group as a result of the intervention, the greatest change is in the area of accountability (See question eight).

Prequestionnaire/Postquestionnaire Comparison of the Focus Group

Question	Focus-Pre	Focus-Post
One	60%	70%
Two	100%	100%
Three	100%	100%
Four	100%	100%
Five	90%	100%
Six	100%	100%
Seven	50%	60%
Eight	0%	40%

Prequestionnaire/Postquestionnaire Questions:

1. When was the last time you shared the gospel with someone?

2. Who is primarily responsible for sharing the gospel? Why?

3. How often are you involved in studying the Bible weekly? (Briefly explain)

4. What is the gospel? (Briefly explain.)

5. What are some of the verses that can be used in sharing the gospel?

6. Who are you currently praying that God will bring to salvation?
7. What are the last four verses you memorized and when?
8. Who regularly holds you accountable to share the gospel? How?

Information from the Exit Interview

The information gained from the exit interview has proven to be very helpful in measuring the success of the project. When asked, why do you believe that most people are not involved in personal evangelism regularly, the majority of the focus group agrees most believers do not understand the responsibility of personal evangelism is for all believers and not just for some supposed spiritually elite. The focus group did note that personal evangelism does not typically fit into one's schedule unless one is **intentional** in his desire to reach the lost. The focus group also mentions sharing the gospel can be uncomfortable. However, each member of the focus group notes how the intervention addresses this issue.

When asked what they learned from the intervention, the group unanimously agrees they all need to be **more intentional** in the area of personal evangelism. Some of the group learned new ways to share the gospel. All realize sharing the gospel is not as difficult as many believe it to be. The group unanimously agrees God is responsible for changing a person's heart and every time they share the gospel, they are successful in their role in personal evangelism. Each member now understands that obstacles to evangelism such as: fear of rejection, fear of not knowing all the answers, fear of failure, etc … are nothing more than excuses. Each member of the focus group agrees with a proper understanding of the role of the believer in personal evangelism and proper training such as the intervention used in this project any Christian can be successful in personal evangelism. This was encouraging to hear!

The entire focus group confesses their need for accountability in personal evangelism. Each member confesses his struggle in this area and agrees that accountability will become a priority in the area of personal evangelism moving forward. **Again, the discipline of accountability appears to be a missing link in consistent personal evangelism.**

During the exit interviews members of the focus group also note many of them are not around unbelievers often because of the time spent in their Christian subculture. Most of the focus group either works at the church or attends a Christian university. Many in the group spend most of their time with other believers. However, they unanimously confess their need to be **intentional** in building relationships with the lost. A few of them even made comments concerning the lesson from John chapter four and how it helps them understand why relationships are so important.

The exit interviews also reveal one necessary change to the intervention. The group members unanimously share that a session to include practicing sharing the gospel is necessary. The teaching is sufficient, however a time to put into practice what is learned would be very helpful in giving those who receive the intervention much needed confidence to go and "make disciples". The project director has filed this information in the must do column for his work moving forward.

CONCLUSION

The United States of America is in a spiritually dark place and the church is losing her influence. It has not always been this way; but the sad reality is that America has seen better days, and the church used to have much greater influence. Max Anders agrees, "The United States is now being described as a post-Christian nation; others say that we are living in a post-Christian world."[148] Spiritual anemia has become the norm. Apathy is the word of the day! Lee Strobel adds, "Most Americans can't even name the four gospels; six out of ten don't know who delivered the Sermon on the Mount. When non-Christians were asked if they knew why Christians celebrate Easter, 46% couldn't give an accurate answer."[149] The spiritual landscape does not look bright. However, light shines the brightest in darkness. The stage is set, and the time is now. The

---

148 Max Anders, *What You Need to Know about Defending Your* Faith. (Nashville, Tennessee: Thomas Nelson Publishers, 1997): 128.

149 Lee Stobel, *Inside the Mind of Unchurched Harry and Mary.* (Grand Rapids, Michigan: Zondervan, 1993): 51.

church must refocus her priorities giving the Great Commission the place it once held in the early church. The early church when faced with great opposition made personal evangelism a high priority. Dr. Luke writes, "Those who had been scattered preached the word wherever they went" (Acts 8:4). Challenge and opposition led the early church to keep the focus on the main thing—sharing Jesus with lost people. The American church of today needs to do the same. Charles Spurgeon writes, "Our main business, brethren, is to win souls."[150] Personal evangelism must be a priority in the church and the priority of every believer. Alphonse Turner adds, "The responsibility to reach those without Christ rests on every Christian."[151] Every Christian needs to understand his responsibility and fulfill his redemptive potential as a minister of reconciliation (2 Cor. 5:11-21). People everywhere who claim Christ must share Him as often as possible with anyone who will listen. The apostle Paul agrees, "However, I consider my life worth nothing to me; my only aim is to finish the race and complete the task the Lord Jesus has given me—the task of testifying to the good news of God's grace" (Acts 20:24). The church can be silent no longer. Those who make it up must live out their faith and share the good news of Jesus Christ with others who are far from God. David Platt writes, "The gospel is the lifeblood of Christianity, and it provides the foundation for *countering culture*."[152] If the

150 Charles Spurgeon, *The Soul Winner*. (Louisville, Kentucky: GLH Publishing, 2015): 16.

151 Alphonse Turner Jr., "A Personal Evangelism Training Plan" (Doctoral diss. Temple Baptist Seminary, Fayetteville, North Carolina, 2013): 76.

152 David Platt, *A Compassionate Call to Counter Culture*. (Carol Stream, Illinois: Tyndale House Publishing, 2015): 1.

church in America is to advance, it must make soul winning a priority. Soul winning will not become the priority of the church until the church makes preparing the members properly in personal evangelism a priority. This is necessary because the gospel is the only news that will bring lasting change to a life, a church, a country, and the world. Jesus has been and forever will be the answer!

Strengths of the Project

Overall, the intervention is a credible source for educating and equipping Christians in the area of personal evangelism. The evangelism workshop (Appendix E) was written in a transferrable format. The workshop was great for the project and is a great resource for any person and for any church. Many of the obstacles to personal evangelism were addressed in the intervention. Tools were given for each member who received the intervention to be faithful and fruitful as a soul winner. All who received the intervention gained a proper understanding of the role of the Christian in soul winning. The greatest changes revealed in the data were in the areas of attitudes concerning personal evangelism and the responsibility of the Christian in the same. There were also some noticeable changes in the actions of certain group members in the area of personal evangelism. These changes are extremely encouraging. **However, for lasting action to remain, it is the conviction of the project director that accountability in personal evangelism must be a part of the process. According to the data, accountability appeared to be a missing link in the focus group concerning the actual practice of personal evangelism.**

Weaknesses in the Project and Future Changes

There were no real weaknesses discovered in the project; however, there are a few additions recommended that will surely increase the effectiveness of the same. One recommended addition to the workshop, as mentioned in the exit interviews of the focus group, is to add a time for the participants to practice the personal evangelism methods taught in the workshop. This can be easily accomplished by adding a little extra time to sessions one and five for the participants to pair off and practice with each other. Additionally, taking the participants to a shopping mall or a public place and encouraging them to share with a stranger would also help solidify the methods of sharing the gospel learned in the workshop. Finally, a time to debrief as a group after sharing the gospel with someone would also be beneficial.

The Transferability of the Project

The project can be easily transferred in two different ways. First, the evangelism workshop (Appendix E) can be taught as a stand-alone workshop. The workshop itself is highly effective and is easily transferrable. It has been taught with great effectiveness in several states and in a few countries. Secondly, the Luther Rice courses (Appendix F) are available online and can be used anywhere in the world at any time. This tool alone is a great resource for any church that is serious about training her people in personal evangelism.

In the spiritual climate of this midwestern city, The First Church (TFC) can continue as normal and see measurable growth. The alarming fact is this growth is and can happen with very little effort in the way of personal evangelism. However, TFC must educate, equip, empower, and encourage its membership to engage in soul winning if she is to witness true Kingdom growth. In order to build an army of personal evangelists, the staff must provide a culturally sensitive discipleship schedule that allows the members to engage in the study of God's Word in the context of their busy lives. Greater attendance in consistent Bible study will result in a greater zeal for personal evangelism. The staff must also preach, teach, and model personal evangelism in their lives, in every area of the church, and with every resource of the church. Thomas Roatch writes, "The preacher who emphasizes the importance of salvation and personal evangelism in his life, sermons and teaching greatly influences his people to win the world to Jesus."[153] It is true, soul winners will lead soul winning churches. Finally, based on the authority of the Lord Jesus Christ, I exhort you to *Go Fish!*

---

153 Thomas M. Roatch, "Effective Personal Evangelism for Today's Church" Doctoral diss. (Liberty Baptist Theological Seminary, 2011): 38.

ABOUT THE AUTHOR

 **Shonn Keels** has spent the last twenty-eight years serving and leading in the local church. He is a lifelong student of leadership and evangelism. Shonn has traveled to six of the seven continents, over thirty countries, and almost every state in the United States sharing the gospel and training church leaders to equip their people to do the same.

Shonn married Bonnie Powell in 1992. They have two adult daughters, Brelin and Baylee. Brelin is married to Bryce Schubert. Bryce and Brelin recently gave birth to Shonn's first grandchild, Indie Eleanor Schubert. Shonn loves spending time with his family. They also have two "fur babies" Mali and Benny.

Shonn received his bachelor's degree from the University of South Carolina in his home state. He continued his studies at

Luther Rice Seminary where he received two masters' degrees and a Doctor of Ministry degree with an emphasis in evangelism.

Shonn is the author of *Maximize your Leadership* and the co-author of *Hold the Rope: Having a Heart for the Lost.* He is also the author of a new eBook, *The Great Debate: Calvinism or Choice.*

Shonn and his family serve together in a local church.

The First Church:
Transfers Vs Baptism

Actual Numbers

Measurements	2013	2014	2015	2016	2017	2018
Avg. Att.	494	512	514	571	660	680
Baptisms	31	23	09	34	25	35
Transfers	73	81	25	104	81	89

6 Year Average Attendance = 572

6 Year Average Baptisms = 26

6 Year Average Transfers = 76

*Most of the baptisms are a result of children's camps, youth camps, and other forms of mass evangelism.

**Very few of the baptisms are a direct result of personal evangelism.

SCRIPTURAL RESOURCES FOR PERSONAL EVANGELISM

Scripture	Evangelist	Recipient
1. Matthew 3:1-2	John the Baptist	Jews
2. Matthew 4:18-22	Jesus	disciples
3. Mark 5:18-20	Legion	people in the town
4. Luke 19:1-10	Jesus	Zaccheus
5. John 1:45-51	Philip	Nathaniel
6. John 4:39	Woman of Samaria	town's people
7. Acts 2:14	Peter	Jews in Jerusalem
8. Acts 3:1-10	Peter and John	lame man
9. Acts 7:1-60	Stephen	Sanhedrin
10. Acts 8:9-13	Phillip	people of Samaria
11. Acts 8:26-39	Phillip	Ethiopian eunuch

12. Acts 8:40	Phillip	People of Azotus
13. Acts 9:10-19	Ananias	Saul
14. Acts 9:20-22	Saul	Jews in Damascus
15. Acts 10:1-48	Peter	Cornelius
16. Acts 11:19-21	persecuted believers	Greeks living in Antioch
17. Acts 11:22-24	Barnabus	believers in Antioch
18. Acts 13:13-43	Paul	People in the Synagogue
19. Acts 16:1-5	Paul	Timothy and the Church
20. Acts 16:11-15	Paul	Lydia
21. Acts 16:27-34	Paul and Silas	prison in Philippi
22. Acts 17:1-9	Paul	those at a synagogue
23. Acts 18:24-26	Apollos	people in Ephesus
24. Acts 18:27-28	Apollos	people in Achaia
25. Acts 27:21-41	Paul	people on a ship
26. Acts 28:16-28	Paul	Jews in Rome
27. Acts 28:30-31	Paul	preached from a house[154]

The Parable Of The Fishless Fishermen

Now it came to pass that a group existed who called themselves fishermen. And lo, there were many fish in the waters all around. In fact, the whole area was surrounded by streams and lakes filled with fish. And the fish were hungry. Year after year these who called themselves fishermen met in meetings and talked about their call to fish, the abundance of fish, and how they might go about fishing. Continually they searched for new and better definitions of fishing. They sponsored costly nationwide and worldwide congresses to discuss fishing and to promote fishing and hear about all the ways of fishing.

These fishermen built large, beautiful buildings called "Fishing Headquarters." The plea was that everyone should be a fisherman and every fisherman should fish. One thing they didn't do, however; they didn't fish. They organized a board to send out fishermen to where there were many fish. The board was formed by those who had the great vision and courage to speak about fishing, to define fishing, and to promote the idea of fishing in far-away streams and lakes where many other fish of different colors lived. Also, the board hired staffs and appointed committees and held many meetings to define fishing, to defend fishing, and to decide what new streams should be thought about. But the staff and committee members did not fish.

Expensive training centers were built to teach fishermen how to fish. Those who taught had doctorates in fishology, but the teachers did not fish. They only taught fishing. Year after year, graduates were sent to do full-time fishing, some to distant waters filled with fish. Further, the fishermen built large printing houses to publish fishing guides. A speaker's bureau was also provided to schedule special speakers on the subject of fishing. Many who felt the call to be fishermen responded and were sent to fish. But like the fishermen back home, they never fished.

Some also said they wanted to be part of the fishing party, but they felt called to furnish fishing equipment. Others felt their job was to relate to the fish in a good way so the fish would know the difference between good and bad fishermen. After one stirring meeting on "The Necessity for Fishing," a young fellow left the meeting and went fishing. The next day he reported he had caught two outstanding fish. He was honored for his excellent catch and scheduled to visit all the big meetings possible to tell how he did it. So, he quit his fishing in order to have time to talk about the experience to the other fishermen. He was also placed on the Fishermen's General Board as a person having considerable experience.

Now it's true that many of the fishermen sacrificed and put up with all kinds of difficulties. Some lived near the water and bore the smell of dead fish every day. They received the ridicule of some who made fun of their fishermen's clubs and the fact that they claimed to be fishermen yet never fished.

They wondered about those who felt it was of little use to attend the weekly meetings to talk about fishing. After all, were they not following the Master who said, "Follow me, and I will make you fishers of men?"

Imagine how hurt some were when one day a person suggested that those who didn't catch fish were really not fishermen, no matter how much they claimed to be. Yet it did sound correct. Is a person a fisherman if year after year he never catches a fish?[155]

---

155 The Parable of The Fishless Fishermen." Chick.com. Chick Publications, May 2000. https://www.chick.com/battle-cry/article?id=Parable-of-the-Fishless-Fishermen.

The First Church: Prayer Requests From Worship 9/15/19

Bettie—Chad and I will be in Tulsa this weekend with my mom; however, Chad has surgery on Wednesday the 18th to begin correcting his knock knees. It's an outpatient procedure and he's expected to feel himself within a couple of days. He will not be able to do sports (he plays hockey), PE, and other similar activities for a few weeks. This will be a particular challenge for Chad because he is such an active athletic guy. He's nervous about his procedure.

Carol—Ashly

Sara—My first cousin, Bill, passed away Saturday.

Edna—Faye is getting a shot tomorrow in her back. Bill is home recovering from surgery.

Geroldien—Please continue to pray for Harvey's healing. His healing seems impossible, but we know God can heal and we continue to pray for total healing. He will be moved from soon.

Jay—Pray for my brother-in-law and sister as he is probably facing an amputation of a foot or leg. He has diabetes, neuropathy, and heart issues. He is not a Christian and won't even discuss it. **(Please notice there is nothing here about praying for this lost person.)** Pray for my sister as she deals with it.

Janice—Dad is moving to a Hospital today. He continues to decline. He is suffering with breathing difficulty. Sister is awaiting tests to see if there's cancer in her kidney. Both kidneys are in poor condition. She needs God in her life. She is resistant to people talking to her about God. **(Still nothing about praying for her salvation.)**

Elizabeth—Thanks for prayers for my son-in-law. He has successfully finished his chemo and radiation.

Patricia—Our President.

LaDonna—Thanks for praying for my friend. Last update: he doesn't have to have surgery. Praise God! The tumor has shrunk since they first found it. They think it is a hematoma from the fall he took. So, in six weeks they will CAT scan or MRI to recheck. Thank you, Jesus.

Frankie—Continued prayer for a friend in her continuing fight against stomach cancer.

Pamela—Continued prayer for friend and his children.

Ronald and Rochelle—Prayer for both of our health.

Jack and Jill—Please pray for my daughter. My son passed away in 2018. This is our second year without him. We are all having a difficult time and I also lost my mother last week.

Gladys—Pray for my brother. He has returned to God.

Jon—I need help praying over my little brother. I just found out from my mom that he is depressed and suicidal.

Sammy—I learned last week that my position as Field Chaplain for a company is ending because of economic conditions. Over fifty people are affected. Please pray for these families as we seek employment.

Rachele—My dad to come to church.

Roger and Mary—A two-week-old, has had a major heart surgery. Pray for his great-grandmother who is with him and his family. Pray for the arrival of a pastor from Uganda. Pray also for my friend's faith struggle.

Grover—My friend's scheduled for hip replacement surgery on Oct 8th.

Lane—Broke my little toe on my left foot. Pray swelling and pain goes down.

Julie—President. Country. Salvation for a friend. Pray for my granddaughter. She is so lost. (**This lady actually asks for the church to pray for salvation!**)

Paul—Pray for my finances, Matthew, marriage, child's-salvation, friend's-salvation, illness, and a friend's abdominal pain. Praise for a friend who is doing well in school.

Jamie—Prayers for strength, guidance, and patience through the week.

Shirl—Thanking God for His love, protection for our church, church staff, and for my health. Please pray for friend, hospitalized with pneumonia, and very low blood pressure. Please pray for another friend as she has been diagnosed with lung cancer and is in hospital. This diagnosis was sudden, and she is dealing with the shock of it.

Dave—My knee. I had an MRI last week. I have an appointment Sept 17 to meet with a doctor.

(All names have been changed to respect the anonymity of those who made these requests.)

Personal Evangelism Workshop Leader's Guide

Suggested Workshop Schedule

Thursday Evening		
	6:30pm—8:00pm	Session One: Change?
Friday Evening		
	6:30pm—8:00pm	Session Two: Biblical Motivations
Saturday Morning		
	9:00am	Session Three: S.A.L.T.
	9:50am	Break
	10:00am	Session Four: L.I.G.H.T.
	10:50am	Break

	11:00am	Session Five: The Gospel
	11:50am	Break
	12:00pm	Session Six: Prayer
	12:50pm	DISMISS

Then Jesus came to them and said, "All authority in heaven and on earth has been given to me. Therefore, go and make disciples of all nations, baptizing them in the name of the Father and of the Son and of the Holy Spirit, and teaching them to obey everything I have commanded you. And surely I am with you always, to the very end of the age."
Matthew 28:18-20

About the Workshop

This workshop includes six sessions designed to enable the student to overcome his fears, develop a strategy for personal evangelism, and step out in faith to share the gospel effectively. Never has there been a time in America so ripe for evangelism. Jesus said, "I tell you, open your eyes and look at the fields! They are ripe for harvest." (John 4:35)

The Six Sessions:

Session 1: Change?
Session 2: Biblical Motivations
Session 3: S.A.L.T.
Session 4: L.I.G.H.T.
Session 5: The Gospel
Session 6: Prayer

The sessions are structured with three elements that will enable the instructor to understand the manual and to teach it effectively.

1. **Clearly Focused Session Plans**. The "Lesson Goals" and "Lesson Focus" enable the instructor to zero in on the important facts to be presented.
2. **Leader Segments**. Each lesson has source materials that illustrate the main points for each lesson.
3. **Creative Group Activities**. This is designed to involve the student in activities that enable him to interact with the principles presented in each session.

> **The fruit of the righteous is a tree of life,**
> **and he who wins souls is wise.**
> **Proverbs 11:30**

Session One: Change?
Lesson Goal
- To evaluate the students' position in Christ

Lesson Focus
- Change, has it taken place and how to communicate this change?

Getting Ready for the Lesson
1. Pray for each student (by name if possible).
2. Study the lesson plan and make notes if necessary.
3. Make sure you have enough necessary materials and supplies for this session.

"But in your hearts set apart Christ as Lord. Always be prepared to give an answer to everyone who asks you to give the reason for the hope that you have."
1 Peter 3:15

Lesson Plan: Session One—Change?

Getting Started (3 minutes)

- Opening remarks
- Announcements
- Prayer

Introduction and Crowd Breaker (12 minutes)

Enlist a few volunteers. Have a couple of them use styling gel to change the hairstyle of one student. Then have the volunteers explain the change from the "old" to the "new" dew.

Transition to Session (2 minutes)

Read 2 Corinthians 5:17 "Therefore, if anyone is in Christ, he is a new creation; the old has gone, the new has come!" **Then say**: If you are to move from the seats and truly impact the streets, the change God has made in your life must be as evident as the change in the "new dew" you just witnessed. And you must be prepared to share this change that has taken place in your life with others.

Session (30 minutes)

Read Luke 19:1-10 and point out the visible change God made in Zacchaeus' life. Secondly, share your personal testimony using the following outline in 5 minutes or less. Then have the students write about the change that God has made in their lives using the same outline below:

1. Life before I <u>surrendered</u> to Christ (3 or 4 sentences)
2. How, why and when I <u>surrendered</u> to Christ (3 or 4 sentences)
3. Life after I <u>surrendered</u> to Christ (3 or 4 sentences)

Closing Remarks (3 minutes)

Encourage the students to practice their testimonies. Have them share their testimonies during session three or four.

Lesson Plan: Session Two—Biblical Motivations

Lesson Goal

*   To encourage the students to develop Biblical convictions in regard to personal evangelism.

Lesson Focus

1. The Call of Christ. Matthew 4:19
2. The Cry of the Lost. Acts 16:22-31
3. The Certainty of Hell. Luke 16:16-31

Getting Ready for the Lesson

1. Pray for each student (by name if possible).
2. Study the lesson plan and make notes if necessary.
3. Make sure you have enough necessary materials and supplies for this session.

"It is not the healthy who need a doctor, but the sick. I have not come to call the righteous, but sinners."
Mark 2:17

Getting Started (3 minutes)

*   Opening remarks
*   Announcements

- Prayer (GO IMMEDIATELY TO VIDEO of the Evangelism Linebacker)

Introduction (5 minutes)

Go to video (https://www.youtube.com/watch?v=lSY1Cl2MQOg)

Transition to Session (3 minutes)

It is not likely that the evangelism linebacker is the one who will really motivate you to share your faith. However, God's word will certainly give you heart-felt convictions about personal evangelism that will lead you out of your seat and into the streets with the life-changing message of the gospel.

Session (see following pages for info on below outline)

1. The Call of Christ (12 minutes)—Matthew 4:19; 28:18-20
2. The Cry of the Lost (12 minutes)—Acts 16:23-31
3. The Certainty of Hell (12 minutes)—Luke 16:22-31

Close session in Prayer (3 minutes)

Pray fervently for God to use His word to motivate all to a life of evangelism and then dismiss to break.

The Call of Christ

Have you heard the Call of Christ?

One author compared the Church's attempt to fulfilling the Great Commission to a professional football contest, a game that consists of 22 men in great need of rest who battle it out while 80,000 others in great need of exercise watch them battle it out. This is unacceptable. The Church of the Lord Jesus Christ has been called and commissioned to go into the entire world with the gospel. Christianity is not a spectator sport! Jesus invited

His earliest followers and so He invites you with the following call, "Come follow me, and I will make you fishers of men" (Matthew 4:19). Please understand this invitation includes both following and fishing. Jesus says those who follow Him will become fishers of men. Have you heard the Call of Christ? Are you fishing?

An old pastor once said, "Imagine how hurt some were when one day a person suggested that those who did not fish were really not fishermen, no matter how much they claimed to be. Yet it did sound correct. Is a person a fisherman if year after year he never goes fishing?"

This is a great place for a personal illustration of how you personally responded to the call of Christ.

Close this point with the question. Have you answered the Call?

The Cry of the Lost

Have you heard the Cry of the Lost?

Tell in your own words the story recorded in Acts 16:23-31. Draw special attention to the response of the jailer, "Sirs what must I do to be saved?" **THEN SAY:** You may never hear someone verbally articulate such a phrase as the jailer did to Paul. However, if you watch the news, read the newspaper, and listen to the people around you, you will hear people crying out in their own words, "Sirs, what must I do to be saved?"

This is a great place for a personal illustration of your hearing someone's cry for salvation.

Close this point with the question. Have you heard the Cry of the Lost?

The Certainty of Hell

Do you believe in the Certainty of Hell?

Read Luke 16:22-31

Tell about the consciousness of the rich man.

Tell how he caught a glimpse of Glory.

Tell how he is still seeking relief today from the agony; but will never receive any relief.

Tell how his destiny is eternally sealed.

Tell how he now wants to be an evangelist.

THEN SAY: Hell is a real place, and many people will go there. You can no longer sit around in your comfortable seat in your air conditioned church while people around you slip into eternity without knowing Christ, the only One who can save them from this real place called Hell. In the next session, you are going to learn how to put these Biblical motivations into practice and with God's help see many of your family, friends, classmates, and co-workers come to faith in Christ.

Pray and dismiss to break.

Lesson Plan: Session Three—S.A.L.T.

Lesson Goal

• To challenge the students to become the "salt of the earth".

Lesson Focus

• To look at the following acronym for S.A.L.T. through the lens of personal evangelism.

Getting Ready for the Lesson

1. Pray for each student (by name if possible).
2. Study the lesson plan and make notes if necessary.

3. Make sure you have enough necessary materials and supplies for this session.

> **"You are the salt of the earth. But if the salt loses its saltiness, how can it be made salty again? It is no longer good for anything, except to be thrown out and trampled by men."**
> **Matthew 5:13**

Getting Started (2 minutes)
- Opening remarks
- Announcements
- Prayer

Introduction (2 minutes)
What is salt good for? (possible answers) Salt is good for: healing, to enhance taste, to preserve things, and to create thirst.

Transition to Session (3 minutes)
In Matthew 5:13 Jesus calls you to be the salt of the earth. He calls you to bring healing to the world, to enhance the taste of life, to preserve the Truth of God's word by passing it along to others, and to create a thirst in others to desire what you have by living a faithful life before them.

Session (see the following pages for info on the below outline)
1. See the Opportunities (10 minutes)
2. Ask Questions (10 minutes)
3. Live like Jesus (10 minutes)
4. Tell about Jesus (10 minutes)

Close session in Prayer (3 minutes)

Pray God will give them the boldness and conviction needed to put these steps into practice.

S.A.L.T.

Are you being the SALT God called you to be?

See the Opportunities

Many want to share their faith. However, they often fail to recognize daily the opportunities around them. Many often see their fellow work associates, classmates, neighbors, family members, and those they pass on the street as nothing more than interruptions to their schedules even though God often puts them in their paths as opportunities. Because of this reality, some of you may need God to heal your sight today. For Jesus said, "lift up your eyes, and look on the fields, for they are white for harvest" (Jn 4:35).

Watch this video and notice that God will often place opportunities before you daily to serve others through intentional relationships. **(Show "Get Service" Video from Sermonspice.com)**

Ask Lots of Questions

Often times people do not share the gospel because they are not sure how to start. Let me suggest you simply start with a question. As you build relationships with those in your circles of influence, you will do well to ask lots of questions and then listen. As you listen, listen for a felt need in the person's life. If you listen long enough, God will eventually give you an opportunity to share the gospel with them. Remember, people don't care what you know until they know that you care. As you listen to them, you earn the right to be heard. **(share a personal example here)**

Live a Faithful Life

Your life speaks so loudly, if not lived faithfully people will not hear what you say. Because your testimony is so important, you must live beyond yourselves and consider others as you make decisions daily. Remember, missions is not just a trip; it is a lifestyle. God has called you to the greatest mission on planet earth, the mission of reaching people with the gospel of Jesus Christ.

Tell them about Jesus

This is where the rubber meets the road. You can talk about evangelism, read about it, study it, and listen to lectures on it for hours at time. However, until you actually talk about Jesus you are not truly involved in evangelism. You cannot fully share the gospel until you open your mouth and tell someone about Jesus. You must tell people about the Good News of Jesus Christ to completely share the gospel.

In the final session you will learn a tool to help you share the gospel clearly and effectively.

Pray and dismiss to break.

Lesson Plan: Session Four—L.I.G.H.T.

Lesson Goal

- To teach the students an effective process of building relationships with those who are far from God and getting to the gospel using the acronym LIGHT.

Lesson Focus
- Lead the students through John chapter four using the acronym LIGHT.

Getting Ready for the Lesson
1. Pray for each student (by name if possible).
2. Study the lesson plan and make notes if necessary.
3. Make sure you have enough necessary materials and supplies for this session.

You are the light of the world. A town built on a hill cannot be hidden. Neither do people light a lamp and put it under a bowl. Instead they put it on its stand, and it gives light to everyone in the house. In the same way, let your light shine before others, that they may see your good deeds and glorify your Father in heaven.

Matthew 5:14-16

Getting Started (2 minutes)
- Opening remarks
- Announcements
- Prayer

Introduction (1 minute)

Sharing your faith can be very scary and confusing. In this session, you are going to learn how to effectively build a relationship with someone who is far from God.

Transition to Session (6 minutes)

Share a personal example of how you built a friendship with a lost person who eventually allowed you the opportunity to share the gospel with him.

Session (20 minutes) Teach the acronym for L.I.G.H.T. using John chapter four.

1. Look for ways to be around someone who is far from God
2. Initiate a growing relationship with this person
3. Get ready for misunderstandings
4. Help them feel loved and accepted
5. Tell them about Jesus

Close session in Prayer (1 minute)

Pray God will give the students the boldness and conviction they need to put these steps into practice.

<u>L.I.G.H.T.</u>

John chapter 4

(An exposition of the below outline can be found in chapter two of *Hold the Rope* by Jeff J. Neal and Shonn Keels and can be purchased on *Amazon*.)

Look for ways to be around people who are far from God

Initiate a growing relationship with the same

Get ready for misunderstandings

Help them feel loved and accepted

Tell them about Jesus

Lesson Plan: Session Five—The Gospel
Lesson Goal

- To teach the students to effectively share the gospel using John 3:16.

Lesson Focus

- John 3:16 one-verse-method (This booklet was written by Dr. Bill Jones and can be ordered from the bookstore at Columbia International University.) You can also download a pdf of this booklet at http://www.bethesdachapel.org/en/wp-content/uploads/2013/02/1a-One-Verse-Evangelism-John-3-16.pdf.

Getting Ready for the Lesson

1. Pray for each student (by name if possible).
2. Study the lesson plan and make notes if necessary.
3. Make sure you have enough necessary materials and supplies for this session.

"I am not ashamed of the gospel for it is the power of God for the salvation of everyone who believes…"
Romans 1:16

Getting Started (2 minutes)

- Opening remarks
- Announcements
- Prayer

Introduction (1 minute)

Sharing your faith can be very scary and confusing. In this session, you are going to learn a simple and effective way to share the gospel.

Transition to Session (6 minutes)

Show the people on the street YouTube video entitled, Purpose of life. You can find this video at: https://www.youtube.

com/watch?v=EGpgt-VENfo **Then say:** Many people miss the purpose of life. The purpose of life can only be found in God through faith in the Lord Jesus Christ. We must introduce people to Jesus.

Session (20 minutes) Teach the John 3:16 one-verse-method

1. God's Plan
2. Man's Problem
3. God's Remedy
4. Man's Response

(After teaching the John 3:16 one-verse-method, have all of the students share it with a partner and vice versa. Give them 10 minutes a piece.) It is also a good idea to send the students out to share with a lost person and then meet again to debrief their experiences.

Close session in Prayer (1 minute)

Pray God will give the students the boldness and conviction they need to put these steps into practice.

Lesson Plan: Session Six—Prayer

Lesson Goal

- To teach the students the importance of prayer in personal evangelism and how to pray for people who are far from God.

Lesson Focus

- Biblical Prayer

Getting Ready for the Lesson

1. Pray for each student (by name if possible).
2. Study the lesson plan and make notes if necessary.

3. Make sure you have enough necessary materials and supplies for this session.

> **"I planted the seed, Apollos watered it,**
> **but God has been making it grow."**
> **1 Corinthians 3:6**

Getting Started (2 minutes)
- Opening remarks
- Announcements
- Prayer

Introduction (1 minute)
God is the Author of salvation. In this last session, you will learn how to pray for people who are far from God.

Transition to Session (6 minutes)
Show YouTube Video on Prayer just for laughs. You can find video at: https://www.youtube.com/watch?v=BkqDpMUu6Yg&t=9s

Then Say: Prayer can sometimes be confusing. However, the Bible clearly give us a roadmap to help us pray for lost people.

Session (20 minutes) Teach on Biblical Prayer
An outline and and key verses included on next page.

Close session in Prayer (1 minute)
Pray God will give the students the boldness and conviction they need to put these steps into practice.

Prayer is the fuel for life and evangelism. We should talk with God about people before we talk with people about God. Therefore, you are encouraged to pray, pray, and pray some more for your students. Also pass along the following Scriptures to your class and encourage them to begin to pray for those they will share with in the future.

(Read these Scriptures together and pray them out loud for specific people.)

Pray that:

- God draws them to Himself. John 6:44
- they seek to know God. Acts 17:27
- Satan is bound from blinding them to the truth. 2 Corinthians 4:4
- strongholds will be demolished. 2 Corinthians 10:3-4
- the Holy Spirit works in them. John 16:8-11
- they believe the Scriptures. 1 Thessalonians 2:13
- God grants them repentance. 2 Timothy 2:24-26
- they turn from sin. Acts 17:30-31
- they believe in Christ as Savior. John 1:12
- they confess Christ as Lord. Romans 10:9-10
- they yield all to follow Christ. 2 Corinthians 5:15

"Call to me and I will answer you and tell you great and unsearchable things you do not know."
Jeremiah 33:3

ONLINE LUTHER RICE COURSES

God is Waiting to Meet You—In this four-session course you will learn the basic character and attributes of God. God has taken the initiative to know you and reveal Himself to you. Through His revelation you find that God is a very personal God who wants you to know Him and has made arrangements for this to be possible. You will not just know about God from watching these videos, but you will be introduced to how you can have a faith-relationship with Him.

Engaging the Word: A Basic Introduction to the Bible— In this four-session course, you will learn basic principles designed to encourage your appreciation for and study of God's Word. We will answer some of the most frequently asked questions by new readers of the Bible, whether you are a new believer, a long-time faithful servant of the Lord Jesus, or a curious seeker. Our hope is to motivate you to dig into the Scriptures for yourself.

Engaging Your Finances—What does God have to say about money management? Is God interested in your financial health? In this four-session course, you will acquire the basic tools for financial management. You will learn that financial health is more than making your money work for you; it is about being a good steward of God's resources.

Engaging the World: A Basic Introduction to Evangelism—In this four-session course, you will learn the basic principles designed to encourage your appreciation for and participation in evangelism. We will answer questions like, "What is evangelism?" "Why should we evangelize?" and "What is successful evangelism?" We will also look at practical ways to evangelize. Our hope is to motivate you to engage the world by sharing your faith with others.

Ready to Engage: A Basic Introduction to Defending the Christian Faith—In this four-session course, you will learn the basic tools designed to encourage you to engage others with and give a reasoned defense of the Christian worldview. We will cover topics like Truth, God's Existence, the Reliability of the Bible, and the Resurrection of Jesus Christ. Our hope is to motivate you to engage the culture with the truth of the Christian faith.

God's Global Purpose—In this four-week course you will consider the following questions. What is God's overarching plan for humanity? Is there one consistent them to Scripture? How does it all fit together in God's grand plan for humanity? You will also be encouraged to think differently about the priority of God's purpose in the Bible and how you fit into it.[156]

---

156 Project Focus | Luther Rice University & Seminary. Accessed September 18, 2018. http://www.projectfocus.education/.

PRETEST-POSTTEST

Please circle your response to the following statements.

1. **Christians regularly participate in personal evangelism.**

   Strongly   Somewhat   Somewhat   Strongly
   Disagree   Disagree   Neutral   Agree   Agree

2. **Christians believe personal evangelism is their respon-sibility.**

   Strongly   Somewhat   Somewhat   Strongly
   Disagree   Disagree   Neutral   Agree   Agree

3. **I participated in personal evangelism within the last week.**

   Strongly   Somewhat   Somewhat   Strongly
   Disagree   Disagree   Neutral   Agree   Agree

4. **Getting a conversion is the responsibility of the one doing personal evangelism.**

   Strongly   Somewhat   Somewhat   Strongly
   Disagree   Disagree   Neutral   Agree   Agree

5. **Personal evangelism is appropriate in a work environment.**

Strongly Disagree   Somewhat Disagree   Neutral   Somewhat Agree   Strongly Agree

6. **I am successful each time I participate in personal evangelism regardless of the listener's response.**

Strongly Disagree   Somewhat Disagree   Neutral   Somewhat Agree   Strongly Agree

7. **I am involved in a regularly scheduled Bible study class outside of Sunday school.**

Strongly Disagree   Somewhat Disagree   Neutral   Somewhat Agree   Strongly Agree

8. **I typically think about the lostness of people.**

Strongly Disagree   Somewhat Disagree   Neutral   Somewhat Agree   Strongly Agree

9. **I read my Bible daily.**

Strongly Disagree   Somewhat Disagree   Neutral   Somewhat Agree   Strongly Agree

10. **I have a lost friend that I pray for daily.**

Strongly Disagree   Somewhat Disagree   Neutral   Somewhat Agree   Strongly Agree

11. **I have a lost friend that I meet with regularly.**

Strongly Disagree   Somewhat Disagree   Neutral   Somewhat Agree   Strongly Agree

PRE-POSTQUESTIONNAIRE

Please answer the following questions. (Use the back of page if necessary.)

1. When was the last time you shared the gospel with someone? (Briefly explain.)

    _____

    _____

    _____

    _____

2. Who is primarily responsible for sharing the gospel? Why? (Briefly explain.)

    _____

    _____

    _____

    _____

3. How often are you involved in studying the Bible weekly? (Briefly explain.)

    _____

    _____

    _____

    _____

4. What is the gospel? (Briefly explain.)

   _____

   _____

   _____

   _____

5. What are some verses that can be used in sharing the gospel? Why? (Briefly explain.)

   _____

   _____

   _____

   _____

6. Who (first name only) are you currently praying that God will bring to salvation? (Briefly explain your relationship to this person or these people.)

   _____

   _____

   _____

   _____

7. What are the last 4 verses you memorized and When? (Briefly explain.)

   _____

   _____

   _____

   _____

8. Who regularly holds you accountable to share the gospel? How? (Briefly explain.)

   _____

   _____

   _____

   _____

Interview Questions For The Focus Group Only

1. Why do you believe most people are not involved in personal evangelism regularly?
2. What did God teach you while participating in this project?
3. What do you believe can make the project more effective in the future?
4. How important is an accountability partner to your involvement in personal evangelism? Why?
5. Why are you sharing the gospel regularly? If not, why are you not sharing the gospel regularly?
6. How often do you pray for lost people or a lost person? Why?
7. What will you do from this day forward to be more faithful in the area of personal evangelism?
8. What are some of the obstacles that keep people from personal evangelism?

COVER LETTER

Dear _____,

I am inviting you to participate in a focus group for my Doctoral Ministry Project on the following dates: January 3-4 (Friday evening through Saturday night). You will also be expected to eat lunch in my home on Sunday, January 26. Lastly, you will be expected to come to my office for a post project one-on-one interview as scheduled between the dates of January 27–31. The project is described in the next two pages entitled "informed consent." The project will take place in my home and a schedule of your commitment is also attached. Please notice that the schedule for the project is similar to a Disciple Now weekend. Below is a list of what you will need for **the weekend.**

List of Needs:

- A Bible
- A pen
- A notebook
- A great attitude and a desire to learn

- Clothes for the entire weekend
- A sleeping bag and a pillow

Please prayerfully read through the informed consent, sign the informed consent, and give it back to me as soon as possible. Your signature of the informed consent is your commitment to willingly participate as a member of the focus group in my Doctoral Ministry Project.

If you have any questions or concerns, please contact me directly at 843-251-1975. Thank you!

Blessings,

Shonn Keels

INFORMED CONSENT[157]

Introduction:

My name is Michael "Shonn" Keels, and I am a student at Luther Rice College and Seminary conducting a study on personal evangelism in the local church for my Doctor of Ministry Project. My telephone number is 843-251-1975. My research supervisor is Doctor Ronald Cobb and his phone number is 770-484-1204 ext. 5684. You may contact either of us at any time if you have questions about this study.

Purpose:

The purpose of this research is to study the practice of personal evangelism in the young adult ministry at The First Church (TFC). I am trying to learn more about the attitudes and actions concerning personal evangelism—sharing the gospel with lost people.

---

157 Mary Clark Moschella, *Ethnography as a Pastoral Practice: An Introduction.* (Cleveland: Pilgrim Press, 2008): 96-97.

Procedure:

If you consent, you will be asked to fill out a pre/posttest, a pre/post questionnaire, and an exit oral interview that will take place in my home. I will document the answers of the pre/posttest and the pre/post questionnaire in a chart and a graph. I may document a transcription of the oral exit interview. I may also document the findings from the answers of the exit oral interview in a graph. You will voluntarily participate in an intense discipleship weekend to be held in my home with ten young adults from TFC.

Time Required:

A copy of the schedule of your participation requirements is attached to this consent form.

Voluntary Participation:

Your participation in this study is completely voluntary. If you choose to participate, you may still refuse to answer any question you do not wish to answer. You may also withdraw from the study at any time.

Risks:

There are no known risks associated with this project. However, it is possible that you may feel distress in the course of the interview. If this happens, please inform me promptly.

Benefits:

While there is no guaranteed benefit, it is possible you will enjoy participation in the project. The study is intended to benefit all participants in the area of personal discipleship and personal evangelism. The result of the study is also intended to benefit TFC and the Kingdom of God for years to come.

Confidentiality/Anonymity:

Your full name will be kept confidential in all of the reporting and/or writing related to this study. I will be the only person present for the oral exit interview and the only person who listens to the recording of the same. When I write the transcription of the interview, I will only use pseudonyms—made up names—for all participants.

Sharing the result:

I plan to use charts and graphs to reveal the results discovered from the project. I may also use a transcription of the oral exit interview. The results will be reported to my research advisor. I also plan to share what I learn from the project with the congregation of TFC. The results will also be shared with Luther Rice College and Seminary and made available to the public for further study.

Publication:

There is the possibility I will publish this project or refer to it in published writings in the future. In this event, I will continue to use pseudonyms (as described above) and I may alter some identifying details in order to further protect your anonymity.

Before you sign:

By signing below, you are agreeing to an audio recording of an oral exit interview for this research project. Be sure that any questions you may have are answered to your satisfaction. If you agree to participate in this study, a copy of this document will be given to you.

Participant's signature ——————— Date: ————

Print name: ————————————————

Researcher's signature ——————— Date: ————

Print name: ————————————————

Selected Bibliography

All Scripture quotations are taken from the New International Version and have been used with permission. The Scripture quotations used can be found on the YouVersion Bible site at www.my.bible.com.

Bible Dictionaries and Commentaries

Baker, William R. et al. *1 Corinthians*. Carol Stream, Ill: Tyndale House Publishers, 2018. *eBook Collection (EBSCOhost)*, EBSCO*host* (accessed August 29, 2018).

Beasley-Murray, G.R. *The Broadman Bible Commentary: Luke—John*. Nashville, Tennessee: Broadman Press, 1971.

Brown, Colin. *The New International Dictionary of New Testament Theology*. Vol. 2 English Language Translation, Grand Rapids, Michigan: Zondervan, 1976.

Brunner, Emil. *The Christian Doctrine of Creation and Redemption*. London: Lutterworth, 1952.

Cole, R. A. *Mark*. Nottingham, England: IVP Academic,
2008. *eBook Collection (EBSCOhost)*, EBSCO*host*
(accessed August 29, 2018).

Edersheim, Alfred. *The Life and Times of Jesus the* Messiah.
Grand Rapids, Michigan: Wm. B. Eerdmans Publishing,
1972.

Hobbs, Herschel H. *The Broadman Bible Commentary: 2
Corinthians–Philemon*. Nashville, Tennessee: Broadman
Press, 1971.

Jones, Bill. *Putting Together the Puzzle of the New Testament*.
Colorado Springs, Colorado: Biblica Publishing, 2009.

Keener, Craig S. *The IVP Bible Background Commentary: New
Testament*. Downers Grove, IL: IVP Academic, 2014.
eBook Collection (EBSCOhost), EBSCO*host* (accessed
August 29, 2018).

Kruse, Colin G. *John*. Nottingham, England: IVP Academic,
2008. *eBook Collection (EBSCOhost)*, EBSCO*host*
(accessed August 29, 2018).

Kruse, Colin G. *2 Corinthians*. Nottingham, England:
IVP Academic, 2015. *eBook Collection (EBSCOhost)*,
EBSCO*host* (accessed August 29, 2018).

Lincoln, Andrew T., David A. Hubbard, Glenn W. Barker, and
Bruce M. Metzger. *Word Biblical Commentary*. Waco, TX:
Word Books, 1990.

Pentecost, Dwight J. *The Words and Works of Jesus Christ*.
Grand Rapids, Michigan: Zondervan, 1981.

Powell, Mark Allan, and Barry L. Bandstra. *The HarperCollins
Bible Dictionary*. New York: Harper Collins, 2011.

Stagg, Frank and Henry E. Turlington. *The Broadman Bible Commentary: Matthew–Mark.* Nashville, Tennessee: Broadman Press, 1969.

Stott, John R. W. *The Letters of John.* Nottingham, England: IVP Academic, 2009. *eBook Collection (EBSCOhost),* EBSCO*host* (accessed August 29, 2018).

Toews, John E. *Romans.* Scottdale, PA: Herald Press, 2004. *eBook Collection (EBSCOhost),* EBSCO*host* (accessed August 29, 2018).

Tolbert, Malcolm O. and William E. Hull. *The Broadman Bible Commentary: Luke—John.* Nashville, Tennessee: Broadman Press, 1970.

Unger, Merrill F. *Ungers Bible Dictionary.* Chicago, Illinois: Moody Press, 1985.

Wiersbe, Warren. *Be Encouraged God Can Turn Your Trials into Triumphs.* Wheaton, Illinois: Victor Books, 1973.

Wiersbe, Warren. *Be Rich Gaining the Things That Money Can't Buy.* Colorado Spring, Colorado: David C. Cook, 1995.

Book References

Aldrich, Joseph C. *Gentle Persuasion: Creative Ways to Introduce Your Friends to Christ.* Portland, Oregon: Multnomah Publishers, 1988.

Anders, Max. *What You Need to Know about Defending Your Faith.* Nashville, Tennessee: Thomas Nelson Publishers, 1997.

Barna, George. *Futurecast.* Carol Stream, Illinois: BarnaBooks, 2011.

Barna, George. *Growing True Disciples.* Ventura, California: Issachar Resources, 2000.

Benavides, Victor H. *Inner City Evangelism.* Alpharetta, Georga: NAMB, 2003.

Berg, Bruce L. *Qualitative Research Methods for the Social Sciences.* 3rd ed. Boston, Massachusetts: Allyn and Bacon, 1988.

Chafer, Lewis Sperry. *True Evangelism or Winning Souls by Prayer.* Findlay, Ohio: Dunham Publishing, 1919.

Chan, Francis. *Crazy Love.* Colorado Springs, Colorado: David C. Cook, 2013.

Clegg, Tom and Warren Bird. *Lost in America: How You and Your Church Can Impact the World Next Door.* Loveland, Colorado: Group Publishing, 2001.

Dickerson, John S. *The Great Evangelical Recession 6 Factors That Will Crash the American Church … and How to Prepare.* Grand Rapids, Michigan: BakerBooks, 2013.

Edwards, Gene. *How to Have a Soul Winning Church.* Springfield, Missouri: Gospel Publishing House.

Godfrey, George. *How to Win Souls and Influence People for Heaven.* Grand Rapids, Michigan: Baker Book House, 1973.

Hybels, Bill. *Courageous Leadership.* Grand Rapids, Michigan: Zondervan, 2002.

Madison, Soyini D. *Critical Ethnography.* Thousand Oaks, California: Sage, 2005.

Maurer, Leon F. *Soul Winning: The Challenge of the Hour.* Murfreesboro, Tennessee: Sword of the Lord, 1970.

McCloskey, Mark. *Tell It Often Tell It Well: Making the Most of Witnessing Opportunities.* San Bernardino, California: Here's Life Publishers.

Moschella, Mary Clark. *Ethnography as a Pastoral Practice: An Introduction.* Cleveland: Pilgrim Press, 2008.

Neal, Jeff J. and Shonn Keels. *Hold the Rope: Having a Heart for the Lost.* New York City, New York: Morgan and James Publishing, 2013.

Patton, Michael Quinn. *How to Use Qualitative Methods in Evaluation.* Thousand Oaks, California, 1987.

Platt, David. *A Compassionate Call to Counter Culture.* Carol Stream, Illinois: Tyndale House Publishing, 2015.

Rainer, Thom. *Effective Evangelistic Churches.* Nashville, Tennessee: Broadman and Holman, 1996.

Rainer, Thom. *The Unchurched Next Door: Understanding Faith Stages as Keys to Sharing Your Faith.* Grand Rapids, Michigan: Zondervan, 2003.

Rainer, Thom and Eric Geiger. *Simple Church.* Nashville, Tennessee: Broadman and Holman Publishing, 2006.

Rainer, Thom. *Surprising Insights from the Unchurched and Proven Ways to Reach Them.* Grand Rapids, Michigan: Zondervan, 2001.

Ravenhill, Ravenhill. *Why Revival Tarries.* Minneapolis, Minnesota: Bethany House, 1987.

Reid, Alvin. *Evangelism Handbook: Biblical, Spiritual, Intentional, Missional.* Nashville, Tennessee: B&H Academic, 2009.

Rhodus, Ronald D. *Local Church Evangelism.* n.p.: 1978., 1978. *COLLIS (Catalog of LutherRice Library Information System)*, EBSCO*host* (accessed August 29, 2018).

Rice John R. *The Golden Path to Successful Soul Winning.* Murfreesboro, Tennessee: The Sword of The Lord Publishers, 1961.

Robinson, Darrell W. *Total Church Life.* Nashville, Tennessee: Broadman & Holman Publishers, 1993.

Russell, Bob. *When God Builds a Church 10 Principles for Growing a Dynamic Church.* West Monroe, Louisiana: Howard Publishing, 2000.

Sensing, Tim. *Qualitative Research.* Eugene, Oregon: Wipf & Stock, 2001.

Spurgeon, Charles. *The Soul Winner.* Louisville, Kentucky: GLH Publishing, 2015.

Stanford, A. Ray. *Handbook of Personal Evangelism.* Pharr, Texas: Wally Marillo, 1999.

Stanley, Andy. *Next Generation Leader Five Essentials for Those Who Will Shape the Future.* Colorado Springs, Colorado: Multnomah Books, 2003.

Strobel, Lee. *Inside the Mind of Unchurched Harry and Mary: How to Reach Friends and Family Who Avoid God and The Church.* Grand Rapids, Michigan: Zondervan, 1993.

Terry, John Mark. *Church Evangelism: Basic Principles, Diverse Models.* Nashville, Tennessee: B&H Academic, 1997.

Wiles, Jerry. *How to Win Others to Christ Your Personal, Practical Guide to Evangelism.* Nashville, Tennessee: Thomas Nelson, 1992.

Academic Journals

Bergler, Thomas E., and Dave Rahn. "Results of a Collaborative Research Project in Gathering Evangelism Stories." *Journal of Youth Ministry* 4, no. 2 (Spring2006

2006): 65. *Advanced Placement Source*, EBSCO*host* (accessed August 29, 2018).

Branum, Josh. "Personal Holiness and Evangelistic Leadership: Understanding the Relationship Between Practicing Spiritual Disciplines and Effective Student Evangelism." *Journal of Youth Ministry* 15, no. 1 (Fall2016 2016): 8. *Advanced Placement Source*, EBSCO*host* (accessed August 29, 2018).

Ford, Leighton. "Personal Evangelism Conversion and Social Change." *The Ecumenical Review* 20, no. 2 (April 1968): 122-130. *ATLA Religion Database with ATLASerials*, EBSCO*host* (accessed August 29, 2018).

Geen, Simon J. "Dr. D. Martyn Lloyd-Jones's Principles of Evangelism with Application for Producing Evangelistic Church Members." *Puritan Reformed Journal* 6, no. 2 (July 2014): 258-269. *Religion and Philosophy Collection*, EBSCO*host* (accessed August 29, 2018).

Keown, Mark J. "Who Were the Evangelisers?: Some Implications of Bauckham's Eyewitness Theory for Early Evangelism." *Stimulus: The New Zealand Journal of Christian Thought and Practice* no. 3 (2016): 24. *Informit Humanities & Social Sciences Collection*, EBSCO*host* (accessed August 29, 2018).

Kosmin, Barry and Ariela Keyser. *"2009 American Religious Identification Survey, Summary."* Hartford, Connecticut: Trinity College, 2009.

Niemandt, C.J.P. (Nelus). "Rediscovering Joy in Costly and Radical Discipleship in Mission." *HTS Theological Studies* no. 4 (2016): 1. *SciELO*, EBSCO*host* (accessed August 29, 2018).

Shoemaker, Samuel M. (Samuel Moor). "Personal Evangelism." *Anglican Theological Review* 29, no. 3 (July 1947): 137-144. *ATLA Religion Database with ATLASerials*, EBSCO*host* (accessed August 29, 2018).

Walker, Alan. "Understanding of Evangelism, and How I Came to It." *International Review of Mission* 64, no. 255 (July 1975): 281-287. *ATLA Religion Database with ATLASerials*, EBSCO*host* (accessed August 29, 2018).

Watson, David Lowes. "Evangelism: A Disciplinary Approach." *International Bulletin of Missionary Research* 7, no. 1 (January 1983): 6-9. *ATLA Religion Database with ATLASerials*, EBSCO*host* (accessed August 29, 2018).

Thesis/Dissertations

Guthrie, David Alexander. "Issues Effecting Church Membership: A Case Study Examining the Vocation of Sharing the Gospel" Doctoral diss. St. Stephen's College, Edmonton, Alberta, GOOGLE, accessed August 29, 2018.

Roatch, Thomas M. "Effective Personal Evangelism for Today's Church" Doctoral diss. Liberty Baptist Theological Seminary, 2011, GOOGLE, accessed August 29, 2018.

Turner, Alphonse Jr. "A Personal Evangelism Training Plan" Doctoral diss. Temple Baptist Seminary, Fayetteville, North Carolina, 2013, GOOGLE accessed August 29, 2018.

Wingate, Dennis Edgar. "Training Believers in Personal Evangelism at Grace Baptist Church, Ridgeway, Virginia"

Doctoral diss. The Southern Baptist Theological Seminary, 2013. GOOGLE accessed August 29, 2018.

Yeich, Stephen Brian. "Christian Perfection as a Vision for Evangelism." Doctoral diss. The University of Manchester 2015, GOOGLE accessed August 29, 2018.

Websites

Barna, George. "Is Evangelism Going Out of Style?" (December 17, 2013). http://www.barna.org/barna-update/article/5-barna-update/53-religious-beliefs-vary-widely-by-denomination (accessed September 12, 2018).

George Barna. "Number of Unchurched Adults Has Nearly Doubled Since 1991." *Barna Group*, May 4, 2004. http://barna.org (accessed September 26, 2018).

Barna, George. "The Most Post-Christian Cities in America: 2017." (July 11, 2017) https://www.barna.com/research/post-christian-cities-america-2017/ (accessed September 12, 2018).

Catt, Michael. "Dr. Chuck Kelley—Southern Baptists Are the New Methodists." October 10, 2012. Accessed September 26, 2018. http://michaelcatt.com/2012/10/dr-chuck-kelley-southern-baptists-are-the-new-methodists/.

Elrod, Brandon. "Evangelism with Johnny Hunt"-NAMB Podcast. Baptist Press. March 06, 2021. https://baptistpress.com/resource-library/news/evangelism-with-johnny-hunt-namb-podcast-launched/.

Havner, Vance. "Vance Havner Quotes." Freedom Christian Quotes. Accessed October 04, 2018. http://christian-quotes.ochristian.com/Vance-Havner-Quotes/.

"Quantitative and Qualitative Research. https://explorable.com/quantitative-and-qualitative-research.

Renfro, Catherine. "5 Steps to Starting Gospel Conversations." On Mission magazine, (Winter 2021). https://issuu.com/namb/docs/omm_winter2021_master_singles/.

"Register for Project FOCUS Online Classes." Project Focus | Luther Rice University & Seminary. Accessed September 18, 2018. http://www.projectfocus.education/.

Shuttleworth, Martyn. "Pretest-Posttest Designs." Explorable, November 3, 2009. https://explorable.com/pretest-posttest-designs.

Shuttleworth, Martyn and Lyndsay T. Wilson. (Jun 16, 2010). Scientific Control Group. Retrieved Oct 18, 2019 from Explorable.com: https://explorable.com/scientific-control-group.

The Parable of The Fishless Fishermen." Chick.com. Chick Publications, May 2000. https://www.chick.com/battle-cry/article?id=Parable-of-the-Fishless-Fishermen.

Wilson, William. "Engaging the World: A Basic Introduction to Evangelism." www.projectfocus.education.

Staff Workshop/Interview

Austin, Jim. Staff Workshop at TFC with Dr. Jim Austin. Retired Executive Director of the South Carolina Baptist Convention, a midwestern city: September 23, 2019.

A free ebook edition is available with the purchase of this book.

To claim your free ebook edition:

Visit MorganJamesBOGO.com
Sign your name CLEARLY in the space
Complete the form and submit a photo of
the entire copyright page
You or your friend can download the ebook
to your preferred device

Morgan James BOGO™

A **FREE** ebook edition is available for you
or a friend with the purchase of this print book.

CLEARLY SIGN YOUR NAME ABOVE

Instructions to claim your free ebook edition:
1. Visit MorganJamesBOGO.com
2. Sign your name CLEARLY in the space above
3. Complete the form and submit a photo
   of this entire page
4. You or your friend can download the ebook
   to your preferred device

Print & Digital Together Forever.

Snap a photo

Free ebook

Read anywhere